Making sanity out of vanity

Making sanity out of vanity

Christian realism in the book of Ecclesiastes

Stanley D. Gale

PUBLISHING WITH A MISSION

EP BOOKS
Faverdale North, Darlington, DL3 0PH, England

web: http://www.epbooks.org
e-mail: sales@epbooks.org

EP BOOKS
P. O. Box 614, Carlisle, PA 17013, USA

web: http://www.epbooks.us
e-mail: usasales@epbooks.org

First published 2011

British Library Cataloguing in Publication Data available

ISBN-13: 978-0-85234-745-4   ISBN-10: 0-85234-745-6

Printed and bound in the USA by Versa Press Inc., East Peoria, IL.

To my grandchildren
— Ruby, Weston, Jasper, Isaac and Kaylie —
that God may grant them a heart of wisdom
from an early age

Acknowledgements

I am particularly indebted to Tremper Longman who gave me the interpretive key to the book of Ecclesiastes in my studies at Westminster Theological Seminary and who later illustrated the use of that key in his book co-authored with Dan Allender, *Breaking the Idols of Your Heart*, which shaped the book you hold in hand. Once again, I am grateful to Mark McCaffrey for his gracious and thoughtful provision of a place to turn thoughts into words. I thank the congregation that I serve as pastor, many who encouraged me in writing a book that developed the sermons they heard on the subject, and for allowing me the time to rest, reflect and write. The book would not be as taut without the exacting eye and incisive comment of my wife, Linda, for whom I am appreciative far beyond her editorial skills. Finally, I'd like to thank Roger Fay, David Woollin, Peter Cooper and Jackie Friston from EP Books for their encouragement and expertise in bringing this book to you.

Contents

For they themselves report
concerning us the kind of reception
we had among you,
and how you turned to God from idols
to serve the living and true God
(1 Thessalonians 1:9).

Foreword

Books from pastors are the best. Pastors handle Scripture carefully, they know us, their affection for people is easy to see, and they know how to make Scripture come to life. That is an unbeatable combination.

Stan Gale is a pastor. He preaches to people he loves every week. Yes, behind his preaching and writing is careful work in the biblical text. He is a devoted student of Scripture. But don't expect those details to be flaunted in this wonderful exploration of Ecclesiastes. Instead, expect a friend — the perfect tour guide — as you look at life 'under the sun'. He will speak *with* you, not *to* you, and certainly not *at* you.

Whatever he tackles is, I believe, worthwhile. I understand he has been preaching through the Minor Prophets, and, if he chooses to write something on those books, I will be sure to read it; but his choice of Ecclesiastes, I believe, is especially timely.

Somehow there is a myth floating around that when you follow Jesus, life has certain tangible perks. When your Father is God and Jesus is the reigning King, you expect that finances won't be quite as tight, relationships will be easier, and life will be a bit merrier. I remember a Christian movie from the 1960s in which I am sure that the main character got better looking once he became serious about Jesus. It was just a little bit of false advertising, provoking seemingly innocent expectations.

Yet these beliefs are far from innocent. When you expect wine and roses and end up with gruel, your confidence in the Lord wanes. Maybe, you wonder, this relationship with Christ is just like a life insurance policy after all. It is good for when you die, but costly while you live. Life insurance policies are boring, at best. Maybe the Bible has no real-world application.

And what about the many men and women who jettison their faith because they encounter suffering — lots of suffering — and following Christ seems to make absolutely no difference? They have been spared nothing. There is a rule in suffering: the more intense the suffering, the more alone you feel from both other people and the Lord. There are times when life is a painful mess, and if God doesn't speak to us in the midst of that mess, why bother?

In Ecclesiastes, God speaks into the mess. Ecclesiastes is not about happy thoughts that deny earthly realities. Instead, the Preacher, along with the other voice we hear in Ecclesiastes, open our eyes even wider than normal. They take us to all the difficult places. They hear our questions and run further with them until all is laid bare. Every once in a while you might think that Ecclesiastes is written by a dour existentialist, but, somehow, even before you get to the end of the book, you can tell that this examination of life will end in hope, and result in more meaning and fulness than we can comprehend.

At the end of Stan's time with you in Ecclesiastes, you won't have a formula for wealth, wisdom or beauty, but you will find comfort, hope and meaning as you know your God is worthy of your complete trust.

Full disclosure. There is another perspective I have on this book that makes it even richer. I happen to know the children who appear in the dedication. They are Stan's grandchildren. Three of them are my grandchildren too. What a comfort it is for me to know that when they are at Pop Pop's house they will be led in this eyes-wide-open wisdom that ultimately not only comes from Jesus Christ but *is* Christ.

Ed Welch

Preface

I first encountered the challenge of the book of Ecclesiastes when I was barely out of the womb of the new birth. God's grace in Christ caught me up when I was a senior in college. I still remember walking the tree-lined campus 'mall' shuffling in my mind all the religious things I had heard growing up but had since found new and real and meaningful — and personal. What to do with my sin? That had become the central question for me, one I had before treated so cavalierly. But now it was the elephant in the room of my heart. Emptiness and alienation felt palpable in the pit of my being.

To that date, a sanitized view of the seriousness of my sin, coupled with a diminished view of the God of the Bible, had given me a false peace, or at least squelched any real sense of need or urgency. But I had been learning more about the grace of God and the cross of Christ, religious concepts whose acquaintance I had made but which I had not come to appreciate.

The stately Dutch elms and halls of learning that surrounded my ruminations as I strolled that college mall became the backdrop to the redemptive drama being worked out in my heart and mind. It became apparent to me what I had to do. I left the mall for my dorm room. Kneeling beside the bed, I committed my life to Jesus Christ, trusting in his work for my salvation, his sacrifice for my sins, bowing to him as Lord of my life.

I had to tell someone. Actually, it was hard for anyone to have a conversation with me without my telling him or her about the wonder of God's love in Jesus. Eventually, my exuberance spilled over to home, ninety minutes from college, where I lived with my grandparents. My grandmother, 'Bam', had been the major religious influence in my life, ensuring I went to a parish church school and was appropriately involved in its activities.

Probably with far too much cockiness and far too little compassion, I pontificated on my newfound experience. Bam was not entirely sure what to make of me but at the very least she saw me as someone invested in the Bible. Over the next few months every visit home would include a tutorial on religious education, with me as the teacher.

On one of those visits Bam told me she was reading the book of Ecclesiastes and it didn't make sense to her. It seemed so depressing, so fatalistic. I'm not sure that was her word, but it was certainly her assessment. To her, the message of Ecclesiastes seemed out of place in the Bible, spoiled fruit among the fresh and delectable cornucopia of God's Word. Knowing that I was now a student of the Bible, the inevitable question came: 'Stanley [grandmothers tend not to use nicknames], what does it all mean?'

I'm sure I had an answer. I always had an answer. If I did not have an answer it might call the Bible into question. I had to defend God. However, I don't remember my response to her. But I can say with certainty now that it would not have been an adequate one, either for a proper understanding of Ecclesiastes or for how God may have been using what she was reading in her life. That would require listening and I did not yet know how to do that when it came to biblical matters, where simply matriculating into Christ's school of discipleship evidently gave me a doctorate at the door. It was through Bam that I was first confronted with the hard sayings of Ecclesiastes, but my response to her was a 'speaking without knowledge'.

Now, many years later, with heightened knowledge and humbled heart, I believe I have come to some understanding of the book of Ecclesiastes and to see what it provides in God's giving it to us and how to bring it to bear to revolutionize life in a fallen world in relationship with God. Ecclesiastes touches every area of life. It is extraordinarily relevant. It keeps it real, a vantage point rejected by unbelief and often revised by believers to make the fallen world conform to narrow categories imposed upon a biblical worldview.

I think it was the late Chuck Daly, one-time coach of American basketball team Detroit Pistons, who said that a pessimist is a realist with experience. Through that voice of experience, Ecclesiastes makes realists of us, a healthy thing for living life in a fallen world. With that realism can come pessimism because the reality we observe and live in, and deal with, appears unfair, arbitrary and hopeless. Even worse, the reality we experience seems to suggest a God who is unfair, arbitrary and helpless, one who is either uninvolved or unconcerned, and maybe even unable.

In my college days as an unbeliever, I soaked up the teaching of atheistic existentialism. I think the philosophy appealed to me in reaction to my religious upbringing; plus it gave me grist for my favourite pastime — arguing with Christians, who often were ill-equipped for the apologetic calling that Peter insists belongs to all believers (1 Peter 3:15). Jean Paul Sartre had the correct view of life as being meaningless and the right answer in making the most of the miserable existence we are all subjected to with nothing more to hope for than death. The writer of Ecclesiastes would sound the 'amen'.

The difference between atheistic existentialism and Ecclesiastes, however, is that the former has legitimate observations but no satisfactory answers, while the God-breathed latter acknowledges the hard reality of it all but offers answers, leading to *the* Answer. In so doing, the perspective of Ecclesiastes is life-transforming and hope-inducing.

So let's embark on a tour of life, both from the vantage point of the jetliner soaring above to survey the whole, and from the navigational challenges of the automobile seeking to negotiate the open highways, hairpin curves and gaping potholes of the road of life.

I do want to interject one important caveat before we embark. This book will be unsatisfying to a reader looking for detailed background information and verse-by-verse exposition of the text. Rather, its aim is not to be a commentary on the book of Ecclesiastes but to use the lens of Ecclesiastes as a practical commentary on life.

Our approach will be to orient ourselves to the book, spreading its map before us and learning its interpretive keys. From there, we'll explore each of the familiar offerings of life, concluding with God's ultimate destination for us.

At the end of each chapter you will find 'Questions from Qoheleth'. Qoheleth is 'the Preacher' of the book of Ecclesiastes, introduced to us in the very first verse, who presents us with many questions but offers few answers. Questions from Qoheleth are not study questions stapled on as an addendum to each chapter, but grow organically from the lesson to amplify and apply. They are intended to lead you to boldly darken the lines traced out in our study to aid in capturing the contours of thought laid out. In addition, they prompt you to add colour within these lines through application to life in general and to your life in particular. Some questions are conducive to group discussion. Some are better answered in the prayer closet. Either way, open yourself now to the searching of the Spirit of God that Christ might be formed in you.

For all our days pass away
under your wrath;
we bring our years to an end like a sigh.
The years of our life are seventy,
or even by reason of strength eighty;
yet their span is but toil and trouble;
they are soon gone, and we fly away
(Psalm 90:9-10).

Introduction
— vanity of vanities

Vanity. van·i·ty/vánitee/n.
  1. conceit about one's appearance or attainments.
  2. futility or unsubstantiality.

'Vanity of vanities! All is vanity' (Eccles. 1:2). That's probably one of the best-known phrases from the book of Ecclesiastes. It opens the book, serves to punctuate it throughout and, lest we somehow missed it, the writer repeats the words at the close of discourse in the last chapter: 'Vanity of vanities, says the Preacher; all is vanity' (Eccles. 12:8). Vanity sets the tone, identifies the problem and lays out the challenge, recorded by God in the Bible in pastoral concern for his people. But what exactly is vanity?

Ordinarily when we think of vanity, we think of quality mirror-time. Singer-songwriter Carly Simon exposes the operating principle of vanity in the line to her 1973 song, 'You're so vain, you probably think this song is about you.' That's the vanity we know, where all roads lead to self. Vanity is about me looking good and wanting others to think so as well.

The vanity mingled among the vanities noted in Ecclesiastes, however, looks more to the second definition of the word given above. When the writer of Ecclesiastes speaks of vanity, he has in mind expressions like empty, meaningless, pointless, hopeless. Like trying to herd a clowder of cats, the effort will be frustrating, the outcome futile. Like trying to get water from a rock, it won't work.

When we apply that to life, vanity speaks to what works and what doesn't. In this sense, Ecclesiastes is eminently practical. It is refreshingly candid in its assessment, mincing no words. Either something works or it doesn't. No spin. No positive light. Just stark reality; as the late sports commentator Howard Cosell would have put it, 'telling it like it is'. That's how Ecclesiastes operates.

Before we put aside the common meaning of vanity, though, the writer of Ecclesiastes would have us pause. The meaning of the word that first occurs to us has to do with self — self-glory, self-absorption, self-service. To be vain is to be myopic to myself. The writer exposes that sort of vanity to be the very conspirator at the helm, foolishly seeking, pursuing that which can never satisfy.

He hints at an insanity to the scope of existence, especially as he tries to discern a divine rational mind at work orchestrating life but is left scratching his head to find rhyme or reason. The colloquial definition of insanity is trying the same avenue and expecting a different result, just what the writer documents as he cites the futility of efforts to find stability, predictability and substance. Vanity of vanities, all is vanity.

In introducing the assessment of 'vanity' the writer of Ecclesiastes prompts us to stop and take notice, to ask questions about our life's ambition and direction, to evaluate how effective and worthwhile are our endeavours, to take a close look at exactly what we are investing in by our time and resources. Behind such assessment looms the question of whose standard we adopt, what makes something worthwhile or not.

Introduction

Life 'under the sun'

'Vanity of vanities' is not alone as a refrain in the book of Ecclesiastes. Other phrases contribute to the recipe of futility and despair. The next one occurring in the book gives us our context, the setting, the milieu for the observations the writer will make in drawing his conclusions of vanity. In the first chapter Ecclesiastes employs the phrase twice.

> What does man gain by all the toil
>   at which he toils under the sun?
>
> (1:3).

> What has been is what will be,
>   and what has been done is what will be done,
>   and there is nothing new under the sun
>
> (1:9).

Ecclesiastes looks at life from an observation deck situated 'under the sun'. What exactly does the writer see? He sees the same things you do. Do you ever scratch your head to wonder why the relationally-challenged and administratively-inept person often gets the promotion over the dedicated and capable person who relates well with others? The writer of Ecclesiastes documents the same thing.

> Again I saw that under the sun the race is not to the swift, nor the battle to the strong, nor bread to the wise, nor riches to the intelligent, nor favour to those with knowledge, but time and chance happen to them all
>
> (9:11).

That's not the way it's supposed to be, is it? The larger army is supposed to emerge as victor in the war. The fastest person is supposed to win the race, right? One of America's bright hopes in the 2008 summer Olympics was Tyson Gay. He held the distinction of reigning world champion in the 100-metre sprint. In the Olympic qualifiers for the 200-metre sprint, he pulled a hamstring and didn't even make it to that event in Olympic competition. The race he *did* run in Beijing, he ended up losing in the semi-finals. When he ran the 400-metre relay, his team dropped the baton. The world's fastest man never even made it to a final in the Olympics. That's more typical of life as we know it. The 'supposed to' of life does not happen as we would expect. That's what the writer of Ecclesiastes describes for us.

It gets even more confusing when we bring God into the picture. We believe in a personal God who is intimately involved in human affairs, whose providence governs all that comes to pass. We believe that God 'works all things according to the counsel of his will' (Eph. 1:11). Yet the writer of Ecclesiastes can see us as victims of time and chance, not beneficiaries of the hand of God in service to the outworking of his plan. When we factor in what we know of a sovereign God who delights to give good gifts to his children, a God who deals in righteousness, who is perfectly just, loving, the God for whom nothing is impossible, we scratch our heads in search of any rational explanation of life's calamities and inconsistencies. Listen to the thought process of Ecclesiastes and hear the confusion, callousness and cynicism.

> In my vain life I have seen everything. There is a righteous man who perishes in his righteousness, and there is a wicked man who prolongs his life in his evildoing. Be not overly righteous, and do not make yourself too wise
>
> (7:15-16).

We observe the same thing as Ecclesiastes as we chart the course of life. The missionary who commits his life to helping others, giving his life for the sake of the gospel, ends up being brutally murdered by those he tries to reach. You would think God's hedge of protection would be especially dense around such a one. Conversely, the despotic dictator who rules his people with an iron fist and seems to indulge in everything counter to God ends up living long and well. Try to make sense of that! That's exactly what the writer of Ecclesiastes challenges us to do — to figure it out. How does reality under the sun mesh with the self-revealed concept of God given us in the Bible? No wonder the writer's bottom line to life is 'vanity' when things don't operate as they should.

I once attended a weeklong meeting where I shared a room with a fellow pastor. In preparation for the trip he had given his electric razor a full charge. The first morning away he stood before the mirror, turned on the razor and … nothing. No buzz. No power. No shave — despite my friend's best-laid plans and preparations to make sure the razor was fully charged before he left home. That exemplifies what the writer of Ecclesiastes sees under the sun. And we sigh the 'amen' as we observe and experience the same thing.

Life under the sun doesn't add up. It defies common sense and contradicts religious sensibilities. Something is amiss.

A broken world

What exactly is this 'under the sun' that serves as the context for what the writer sees, the matrix for the outworking of life? Genesis 3 gives us the background. With Adam's disobedience, all the created order fell under the dominion of sin. Sin polluted, perverted and damaged everything. The world became dysfunctional. Weeds grew. Anger festered. People killed. Like dark, billowing clouds blot out the warmth and light and beauty of the sun, the glory of God became obscured and the normalcy of people in relationship with God became abnormal, even adversarial.

That's what the writer of Ecclesiastes observes. The Fall, as recorded in Genesis 3, is no mere page of dry history or ephemeral theological concept. It's where we live and move and have our being. What the writer records in his observations of life is a diary of our own existence expressive of frustration and splotched with tears.

'A striving after wind'

Ecclesiastes uses one other phrase to capture life under the sun, one that describes what it's like to try to find meaning, purpose, value and identity in a fallen world. Not only do we observe senselessness and emptiness as we look at life but, like with my friend's razor, when we try to get somewhere with the world's offerings we find them powerless and pointless. The writer's commentary drips with existential angst.

> Enjoy life with the wife whom you love, all the days of your vain life that he has given you under the sun, because that is your portion in life and in your toil at which you toil under the sun
>
> (9:9).

Sartre would be proud. That's the way to get through life. You just enjoy what you can, try to make the most of things, meagre as it is, and you die. Much of life's offerings are nothing more than anaesthesia, dulling the pain of a meaningless existence, or distractions keeping us from becoming overwhelmed by the senselessness and hopelessness of it all.

The writer of Ecclesiastes expresses this as a 'striving after wind'. Twice he employs the expression in the opening chapter.

> I have seen everything that is done under the sun, and behold, all is vanity and a striving after wind
>
> (1:14).

> And I applied my heart to know wisdom and to know madness and folly. I perceived that this also is but a striving after wind
>
> (1:17).

Could a phrase better express the futility to life than 'striving after wind'? You can't see what you're doing. You can't do what you're trying to do. And why bother in the first place? Life under the sun is played out on a merry-go-round, where you are ever-moving but never getting anywhere, the hope of the brass ring supposedly present by design but rarely found and seemingly always out of reach. We might think of Sisyphus, struggling to push the rock up the mountain, only to have it tumble back down. Frustration, futility and folly — those are the earmarks of efforts under the sun. And where does faith fit in? No wonder my grandmother was confused. She's not the only one!

Redemptive reality

Yet as pessimistic as Ecclesiastes seems, we actually find it a place of great hope and spring of life. The observations it makes are real and they are sobering. The answer, though, is not to find the silver lining or hope for better days or to settle for some semblance of sanity. The answer to the pessimism is not contrived optimism through positive spin or pious platitudes. The answer is redemptive reality.

Back when colour television was just making its way into homes, as a pre-teen I was desperate to have one. My family, though, did not share my zeal. Determined, I noticed in the back of one of my comic books the solution to my problem. There was an advertisement for a product to turn my TV's black and white picture into full and living colour. I ordered it without delay. When it arrived in the promised six to eight weeks, I tore open the package to discover a translucent film with directions to cut it to the size of my television screen and place it over the top. The film had three parallel bands of colour, blue at the top, yellow in the middle and brown at the bottom. The sad part of the story is that I was actually happy with it, convincing myself it made a difference. We can employ the same tack in dealing with life under the sun, denying reality or dressing it up in an effort to make it something it is not.

Here's where we find the genius and hope of Ecclesiastes, not in denying reality but in redeeming it, where 'under the sun' holds the harsh reality but not the answer. The answer is not found in reformation but in transformation and that not in ourselves but by the redemptive plan and hand of God. In a seeming senseless and irrational world, Ecclesiastes allows us to make sanity out of vanity.

Questions from Qoheleth

1. What three phrases do we find repeated in the book of Ecclesiastes? What does each mean and how do they relate to one another to convey the tone of the book?

Introduction

2. What two meanings does the dictionary give us for 'vanity'? Which one does the writer of Ecclesiastes mean? How can the other definition relate to the message of the book?

3. What is the relationship of vanity to insanity, especially when we consider that God directs life?

4. What is an example from your own life, from the life of someone you know, or from current events, that could find its way into the pages of Ecclesiastes? How does this example promote cynicism? If you were to give voice to that cynicism what are some things it might say?

5. What is the background to the phrase 'under the sun'? How does Romans 1:18-23 help us to understand the origin of the futility we experience under the sun?

6. What are some ways we try to cope with life? Apply these ways to a recent example of a struggle you have had with making sense of some circumstance. How does the story of the 'colour' television illustrate efforts to cope with life?

7. What is NOT the answer to the pessimism, scepticism and cynicism of the Preacher? What IS the answer? Why do we tend to align ourselves with the Preacher?

8. Knowing that God gives the books of the Bible in pastoral concern for us (i.e., they were not dropped down as oracles but spoken to our redemptive need), why do you think God included Ecclesiastes in the Bible? How does it function to make us realists? What value is there in our being realists in our approach to life?

9. What would you say to someone who pointed out that Ecclesiastes is negative and presents a message contrary to the message of the Bible?

10. Read Psalm 90. How can it function as a prayer for embarking on a study of Ecclesiastes and application of its message?

[Wisdom] has sent out her young women to call
from the highest places in the town,
'Whoever is simple, let him turn in here!'
To him who lacks sense she says,
'Come, eat of my bread
and drink of the wine I have mixed.
Leave your simple ways, and live,
and walk in the way of insight.'

The fear of the LORD is the beginning of wisdom,
and the knowledge of the Holy One is insight.

The woman Folly is loud;
she is seductive and knows nothing.
She sits at the door of her house;
she takes a seat on the highest places of the town,
calling to those who pass by,
who are going straight on their way,

'Whoever is simple, let him turn in here!'
And to him who lacks sense she says,
'Stolen water is sweet,
and bread eaten in secret is pleasant.'
But he does not know that the dead are there,
that her guests are in the depths of Sheol

(Proverbs 9:3-6, 10, 13-18).

1.
Vanity Fair

Then I saw in my dream, that when they were got out of the wilderness, they presently saw a town before them, and the name of that town is Vanity; and at the town there is a fair kept, called Vanity Fair: it is kept all the year long. It beareth the name of Vanity Fair because the town where it is kept is lighter than vanity; and, also because all that is there sold, or that cometh thither, is vanity. As is the saying of the wise, 'all that cometh is vanity.'

This fair is no new-erected business, but a thing of ancient standing; I will show you the original of it.

Almost five thousand years agone, there were pilgrims walking to the Celestial City, as these two honest persons are; and Beelzebub, Apollyon, and Legion, with their companions, perceiving by the path that the pilgrims made, that their way to the city lay through this town of Vanity, they contrived here to set up a fair; a fair, wherein should be sold all sorts of vanity, and that it should last all the year long; therefore at this fair are all such merchandise sold, as houses, lands, trades, places, honours, preferments, titles, countries, kingdoms, lusts, pleasures; and delights of all sorts, as whores, bawds, wives, husbands, children, masters, servants, lives, blood, bodies, souls, silver, gold, pearls, precious stones, and what not

(Bunyan, *Pilgrim's Progress*).

Making sanity out of vanity

In his classic work, *Pilgrim's Progress*, John Bunyan escorts us to Vanity Fair. The Fair, he says, is open for business year round. And it's not a new business, but was established from ancient times. The Fair offers all the wares and services typical to mankind, some inherently dishonourable, some not. But all the offerings share a common description — they are vanity.

This sounds like a page right out of Ecclesiastes.

> And whatever my eyes desired I did not keep from them. I kept my heart from no pleasure, for my heart found pleasure in all my toil, and this was my reward for all my toil. Then I considered all that my hands had done and the toil I had expended in doing it, and behold, all was vanity and a striving after wind, and there was nothing to be gained under the sun
>
> (Ecclesiastes 2:10-11).

We all agree that work is good in God's eyes, don't we? How then can it find a place in Vanity Fair among 'lusts, blood and bawds'? Marriage, money and homes are good things, aren't they? How is it they are listed by Bunyan on the directory of marketplaces of Vanity Fair? Like 'gentlemen's clubs' and 'exotic dancers', we can understand how undesirables and depravities set up shop in the Fair and attract those like them. But children and possessions! — What place do they have among the unsavoury and immoral?

The point is that even that which is good and noble can be corrupted and misused. The knife that saves life on the surgeon's table can be used to take it by the hand of rage. Family is a good thing, a blessing of God to be protected and nurtured. Yet when family becomes an end in itself, a substitute for God, it then finds its place in the aisles of Vanity Fair.

Who is the proprietor of Vanity Fair? Bunyan identifies a partnership of Beelzebub, Apollyon and Legion. These three are one, a sampling of names given in the Bible, identified for us by God as the prince of this fallen world, the god of this age, whose goal it is to prompt us to indulge in that which is false, having an appearance of worthiness, even godliness, but is a vain offering, devoid of power for life.

We find Satan's first sales pitch at the dawn of humanity amidst the backdrop to which we referred earlier.

> Now the serpent was more crafty than any other beast of the field that the LORD God had made. He said to the woman, 'Did God actually say, "You shall not eat of any tree in the garden"?' And the woman said to the serpent, 'We may eat of the fruit of the trees in the garden, but God said, "You shall not eat of the fruit of the tree that is in the midst of the garden, neither shall you touch it, lest you die."' But the serpent said to the woman, 'You will not surely die. For God knows that when you eat of it your eyes will be opened, and you will be like God, knowing good and evil'
>
> (Genesis 3:1-5).

The devil hawks a vain thing, something appealing to the senses, even sensible to the independent mind, but empty of promise and destructive to life, a placebo at best, a poison at worst.

A similar theme and call for discernment of 'buyer beware' echoes throughout the pages of Holy Writ. Psalm 1 enjoins us to distinguish between competing counsel of wisdom and folly, displaying for us the lot of each path. Proverbs 9 records the invitations of Lady Wisdom and Dame Folly, both situated by the way, both appealing to those who seek sense amidst the vanity of life, yet each leading to its own end, wisdom to richness of life, folly to death itself: 'But he does not know that the dead are there, that her guests are in the depths of Sheol' (Prov. 9:18). There is a way that seems right to a man, the proverb cautions us, but its end is the way of death. Like grocery shopping on an empty stomach, we need to be guarded and discerning in our purchases, knowing the folly to which we are prone.

The theme of discernment for those living in the midst of Vanity Fair continues in the New Testament, from Jesus' caution in Matthew 7:24-27, urging us to be careful where we build our house, to the sobering words of the apostle Paul:

Therefore, as you received Christ Jesus the Lord, so walk in him, rooted and built up in him and established in the faith, just as you were taught, abounding in thanksgiving. See to it that no one takes you captive by philosophy and empty deceit, according to human tradition, according to the elemental spirits of the world, and not according to Christ

(Colossians 2:6-8).

Perhaps no better passage lays it on the line for us in the face of the lures of Vanity Fair than God's words through the prophet Isaiah.

'Come, everyone who thirsts, come to the waters; and he who has no money, come, buy and eat! Come, buy wine and milk without money and without price. Why do you spend your money for that which is not bread, and your labour for that which does not satisfy? Listen diligently to me, and eat what is good, and delight yourselves in rich food. Incline your ear, and come to me; hear, that your soul may live; and I will make with you an everlasting covenant, my steadfast, sure love for David'

(Isaiah 55:1-3).

The lines of communication to which we are to listen run throughout Scripture, taking us to the highpoint of the Mount of Transfiguration: 'This is my beloved Son, with whom I am well pleased; listen to him' (Matt. 17:5).

The market of Vanity Fair may offer milk and bread but its calories are empty and nutrients non-existent. Against the din of Satan's incessant shouts urging us to enter the shop and spend the currency of our labours according to the acumen of our own assessments, the counsel of God directs us to listen to him, eat what is good, delight ourselves in what will truly satisfy and find life itself, ultimately through his covenant faithfulness realized in the Son of David, in whom is bound the wisdom of God.

It should be apparent by now that Vanity Fair is spread before us 'under the sun', its wares a vain offering, 'lighter than vanity', as Bunyan puts it; expressed by the Preacher as 'vanity of vanities', the emptiest of empties. Ecclesiastes escorts us through the aisles of Vanity Fair, pointing us as a tour guide through a marketplace of alleged answers to life, means to fulfilment, escapes from the angst of a frustrating life, which fill the shelves waiting for purchase. But, as a father taking his child by the hand, our God takes our hand in his to guide us through the shams and scams of life under the sun with the goal of finding life, hope, meaning and purpose in him, arrived at through heeding his words recorded in Isaiah that we listen intently to him.

In this tour conducted by Ecclesiastes we are exposed to virtually every area of life in which we might seek to find sense and significance at the behest of the hawkers of Vanity Fair: family, friends, money, possessions, sex, entertainment, education, status, religion, social causes, physical fitness and beauty. Throughout, Ecclesiastes alerts us to the folly and shows us how to reclaim life from the vanity under the sun that we might be kept from striving after wind, and instead may find where our life and labour are not in vain.

Questions from Qoheleth

1. In John Bunyan's *Pilgrim's Progress*, where was Vanity Fair held? What do you think lies behind that name? Why would Bunyan speak of a fair being there? What do you notice about this fair? What parallels can you draw between the town and its fair and the world in which we live?

2. Who are the proprietors of Vanity Fair? What does the New Testament's background check tell us about this management team (e.g., John 8:44; 2 Cor. 11:3; Eph. 2:1-3; 1 Peter 5:8; Rev. 2:9)? Why should this put us on guard in the course of life? To what should we particularly be on the alert?

3. How can the Bible itself be found in the library of Vanity Fair? How do we improperly use the Bible? Why are Christians sometimes charged with 'bibliolatry'? How does the devil twist God's Word in Genesis 3:1-5 and Matthew 4:1-10?

4. How can something take the place of God in our lives? What does that look like in practical terms?

5. What are examples of things or activities that are not bad in themselves but can be corrupted and misused? How is the fruit of the tree in Genesis 2:17 an example of this?

6. Read Proverbs 9, verses 4 and 16. What is the appeal? To whom is it made? Who is making the appeals? What are the consequences of listening to and following each appeal in Proverbs 9:6 and 9:18? How does this relate to life for us in this world of Vanity Fair?

7. What two ways are contrasted in Psalm 1? In Colossians 2:6-8? In Isaiah 55:1-3? How does Ecclesiastes present the same contrast?

8. Knowing we live in a world filled with counterfeit offerings, what is our need (see Prov. 17:24)? How relevant is Psalm 119:33-40 as a daily prayer in this need?

9. What offerings of Vanity Fair do you think you may have bought into? What is God calling you to do with them? How does Ephesians 4:17-24 instruct you to follow God's call?

*Trust in the L*ORD *with all your heart,*
and do not lean on your own understanding.
In all your ways acknowledge him,
and he will make straight your paths.
Be not wise in your own eyes;
*fear the L*ORD, *and turn away from evil.*
It will be healing to your flesh
and refreshment to your bones

(Proverbs 3:5-8).

2.
Making sanity out of vanity

'Be not overly righteous, and do not make yourself too wise'
(Eccles. 7:16).

'Bread is made for laughter, and wine gladdens life,
and money answers everything'
(Eccles. 10:19).

Be honest. Would you have identified those as quotes from the Bible? No wonder Bam was confused. Statements like these seem anti-Bible, contrary to the things God desires. What do we make of them?

How do we make sanity out of vanity? How do we make sense out of seeming senselessness? How do we make rhyme or reason out of a world that appears to be spiralling out of control, especially as we believe that God's perfect and powerful hand of providence governs all that comes to pass? How can we face the pain and frustrations of life head on, without denial or escape? More than that, how can we actually go about finding life and fulness and delight in our days under the sun?

At first it seems that Ecclesiastes offers us no help in finding sense and sensibility in a confusing and chaotic life. In fact, it only seems to muddy the waters.

Making sanity out of vanity

> There is an evil that I have seen under the sun, and it lies heavy on mankind: a man to whom God gives wealth, possessions, and honour, so that he lacks nothing of all that he desires, yet God does not give him power to enjoy them, but a stranger enjoys them. This is vanity; it is a grievous evil
>
> (6:1-2).

What kind of God does things like that? It's like a father offering his son his favourite candy bar, only to give it to someone else.

On the one hand we read passages like these and we breathe a sigh of relief:

> Though a sinner does evil a hundred times and prolongs his life, yet I know that it will be well with those who fear God, because they fear before him. But it will not be well with the wicked, neither will he prolong his days like a shadow, because he does not fear before God
>
> (8:12-13).

That's the way it's supposed to be. That's what we would expect in a just, fair and righteously rational world. But then we go on and read passages like that which immediately follows and we scratch our heads in total confusion:

> There is a vanity that takes place on earth, that there are righteous people to whom it happens according to the deeds of the wicked, and there are wicked people to whom it happens according to the deeds of the righteous. I said that this also is vanity. And I commend joy, for man has no good thing under the sun but to eat and drink and be joyful, for this will go with him in his

toil through the days of his life that God has given him under the sun

(8:14-15).

That's it? That's the best the wisdom of Ecclesiastes can offer us, flaunting contradictions and magnifying meaninglessness? Yes — and no. Pointing out the insanity sets up a didactic device to drive home God's lesson for us.

Two voices

In the days of my childhood, games were a bit simpler before the advent of sophisticated electronic games. One game I had as a boy provided a clever way of concealing and revealing answers to questions. The answer key would have black and red on it. It was virtually impossible to discern the answer embedded amidst the squiggles. However, when a sheet of red film was placed over the answer key, only the black could be seen, thus exposing the answers. Without that sheet of red film the answers remained in plain sight but hidden to the eye.

Ecclesiastes operates in similar fashion. The book does equip us to find our bearings and direct our steps, but it requires an answer key. God himself provides that key for us within the book itself that serves as the interpretive grid for understanding both the book and the life it observes.

If we look closely at Ecclesiastes we find two voices from the hand of a single author. The bulk of the book is written in the first person singular: 'I saw, I applied, I said, I searched, I considered, I made,' etc. The portion written in the first person extends from Ecclesiastes 1:12 to 12:7.

The 'I' referred to in Ecclesiastes comes from one identified as 'the Preacher'. Some translations do not translate the Hebrew word but just transliterate it, giving the Hebrew letters an English equivalent, rendering 'the Preacher' as Qoheleth. Qoheleth means collector, and it becomes obvious why the title fits. He is an observer of life, a collector of snippets and scenarios under the sun. More than that, he is a religious observer of life, factoring in God and morality and justice. The Preacher brings a religious framework to bear that looks at life and tries to make sense of it, much like we do as we try to figure out what God is doing in the course of human events or what we think he should do according to the rules of operation we understand from his Word. From this perspective the Preacher draws conclusions and makes commendations in his scrapbook on life.

However, we hear a second voice in the book of Ecclesiastes. This voice comes to us not in the first person of the Preacher, but, rather, is recorded in the third person and speaks *about* the Preacher and his observations. Listen to the two voices that come to us in the first chapter, hearing, first, the voice of the Preacher himself, and then the voice in the third person speaking about the Preacher.

I the Preacher have been king over Israel in Jerusalem. And I applied my heart to seek and to search out by wisdom all that is done under heaven. It is an unhappy business that God has given to the children of man to be busy with. I have seen everything that is done under the sun, and behold, all is vanity and a striving after wind

(1:12-14).

The words of the Preacher, the son of David, king in Jerusalem. Vanity of vanities, says the Preacher, vanity of vanities! All is vanity

(1:1-2).

Making sanity out of vanity

Unlike the voice of the Preacher, the voice of the other speaker is not given a name. He is portrayed as an unnamed father teaching his son against the foil of the Preacher who looked to instruct the masses.

> Besides being wise, the Preacher also taught the people knowledge, weighing and studying and arranging many proverbs with great care. The Preacher sought to find words of delight, and uprightly he wrote words of truth.
> The words of the wise are like goads, and like nails firmly fixed are the collected sayings; they are given by one Shepherd. My son, beware of anything beyond these
>
> (12:9-12).

This teacher could be a father instructing his son or he could be a teacher educating his disciple in the way of wisdom. The unnamed teacher's voice brackets the first person observations of the Preacher (1:1-11; 12:8-14).

As we can see in Ecclesiastes 12:9, the teacher explains to his disciple the Preacher's endeavour to collect and instruct. He describes the Preacher's well-intentioned wrestling with the reality in what he observed under the sun. The teacher commends the Preacher's effort and affirms the authenticity of his observations. It's true, the righteous do falter; the wicked do prosper. The race is often not to the swift. Honest, hard work frequently ends with nothing to show for it. It does appear that God is unpredictable and that life smacks of irrationality, apparently with no sane Sovereign orchestrating it. The Preacher calls it like he sees it and the teacher tells his disciple that the Preacher sees it as it is.

But — and here's the translucent red sheet, the interpretive key — there's another way to look at life. The Preacher limits himself by looking at things under the sun and drawing his conclusions from the constraints of that vantage point. He understandably becomes cynical as he sees a world run amok under the ravages of sin by virtue of the Fall. How can one not become a sceptic by looking at the frustration and futility that abound? It's like reading the accounts of murders, wars and crime in the daily newspaper and not being jaded, even calling into question the character and involvement of God. It's true. It's real. Now, what does it mean? How are we to understand it all? More than that, how do we live in that setting?

It reminds us of the book of Job as he tried to deal with the death of his children and loss of possessions. Job asked similar questions: 'Why do the wicked live, reach old age, and grow mighty in power?' (Job 21:7). Job was never given answers. Rather, he was presented with the majesty and mystery of God, who did have answers, and was told to rest in him. Ecclesiastes takes the same approach. We might not be able to figure it all out, but the teacher instructs us in what we can do in whatever we face:

> The end of the matter; all has been heard. Fear God and keep his commandments, for this is the whole duty of man. For God will bring every deed into judgement, with every secret thing, whether good or evil
>
> (12:13-14).

The teacher affirms the reality of what the Preacher observes under the sun, but he takes his son, and us with him, beyond the created order under the sun, now fallen and messed up and subjected to futility, and lifts our eyes to the Creator and our relationship with him and responsibility to him in navigating the paths and pitfalls of life in that fallen world. More than that, we can superimpose the lens to life offered by the teacher to find *legitimate* delight and *proper* significance in all those dimensions of life observed by the Preacher, whether it be family or work or religious endeavour.

Fearing God

What does it mean to 'fear' God and what bearing does that have on life under the sun? It has everything to do with our existence and the vanity we experience and the quest for meaningful pursuits. Fearing God means ascribing to him the glory due his name. It means living in the light of God's revealed character, despite appearances to the contrary. Cynicism operates on the basis of a false god, a contrived god, a god manufactured by our estimations. Fearing God reaches beyond the distortions of the fallen world to appropriate the revelation of the true and living God and to operate on the basis of that knowledge. Fearing God acts to regard a God who created all that is, who continues to reign over all that is, and who is at work in all that is for his purposes and goals.

Fearing God keeps us from seeking to find meaning and purpose in the wares of the world that will always disappoint and never ultimately satisfy. Fearing God is willingness to accept confusion, frustration and conflict because it embraces its humanly limitations and sin-skewed sensibilities and works to know and trust the God who is wholly other. Fearing God adopts a vantage point to life beyond the fallen created order under the sun, and a posture for relating to God in the midst of it.

Instead of trying to find meaning in the world, fearing God finds meaning in God. Fearing God involves a tenacity to cling to God, trusting him because it walks by faith in what God has revealed about himself. Fearing God tolerates no substitutes for God, looking to created things for what can be found only in God and in relationship with him.

'Fear God and keep his commandments,' the unnamed teacher counsels his charge. Fearing God speaks to a God-*centred* life. Obeying his commandments addresses a God-*serving* life. Our God is the terminus of our striving. Our God is the substance of our living. Our God is the answer to the futility we face under the sun, where our confusion is allayed by resting in his will and our frustration is remedied by finding fulness in his means. This interpretive key touches upon and transforms every area of life, reclaiming each dimension of the Preacher's inventory, infusing it with proper meaning and regulating its proper use for the glory of God.

Finding hope

Often as Christians we can live our lives (or at least try to) with rose-coloured glasses. Ecclesiastes rips those rose-coloured glasses off us. It is written to make realists of us. It makes us come to grips with life in a fallen world, a world full of suffering and miseries and religious non sequiturs, a world turned upside-down and inside-out from the incident in Eden.

Unbelievers shackled with blinders under the sun scoff at the notion of a sovereign God who is all powerful and all good. They say, 'Look at the famine, the wars, the injustice.' We often put up a brave front, but we have the same questions. 'If I'm trying to do the right thing, then why doesn't God help me? It seems he's toying with me. Something positive happens and I say, "Thank you, God," but then he takes it away. I just don't understand.' Or, 'Why am I constantly second choice for the job opportunity. Doesn't having God as my Father count for something?' And our enemy, the devil, whispers not only 'Did God really say?' but 'Is God really good?'

Ecclesiastes, a book that doesn't seem to make sense, actually is given us by God to help us to make sense as we navigate the pathways of this fallen world. We read the book of Ecclesiastes, just like we read the pages of everyday life, and we say, 'Why bother? What's the use? I don't get it.' It seems to rip away any firm footing, and hope. And that's exactly what it does. It rips away the hope we try to find in the *wrong* places, so that we can find hope where only hope can be found — not in the offerings and avenues of a fallen world under the sun, but in God and his redemption in Jesus Christ, who came that we might have life and have it abundantly. In other words, Ecclesiastes is intended not only to make us realists; it is intended to make us *redemptive* realists, finding meaning, purpose and fulfilment in the hope that is ours in Jesus Christ.

Now we embark on a tour of Vanity Fair, looking at ways we might try to find substance and significance in those offerings under the sun, or might try to find escape and diversion from the harshness of life under its withering, disorienting intensity. Beside us at every point is the proprietor of the fallen world with his seducing spiel and counterfeit offerings, but with us is the Spirit of God in the interpretive grid of his Word giving each offering its place and sanctifying it for our use, transforming the vaporous and vacuous life the Preacher observes into one that is vibrant and verdant in Jesus Christ.

Questions from Qoheleth

1. What are some examples of how life challenges our conception of God? Being honest with yourself, how have you experienced what the Preacher observes in Ecclesiastes 6:1-2?
2. What are the two voices we find in the book of Ecclesiastes? How do we recognize each voice? How do the voices relate to one another?
3. What does the word translated 'the Preacher' mean? In what way can he be called a preacher?

4. How does the unnamed teacher use the Preacher's observations? Does he agree with the Preacher's conclusions? Why or why not? How might we teach our children in Sunday School or home in a fashion similar to the approach of the teacher?

5. If the Preacher makes his observations under the sun, what perspective does the unnamed teacher introduce? How does the teacher look at the same things as the Preacher but draw different conclusions? What is an example of a different take you have from an unbeliever on the same circumstance?

6. What does it mean to fear God? How does fearing God relate to faith? How does fearing God affect our view of self?

7. In what way is fearing God foundational to keeping his commandments? What happens when we look to obey without fearing God?

8. How does Proverbs 3:5-8 instruct us in fearing God? In what way is Proverbs 3:9-10 an illustration of that instruction? How is the fear of God the fountain of true wisdom (cf. 1 Cor. 3:18-20)?

9. Fill in the blanks: fearing God speaks to a God-_____ life; obeying God's commandments speaks to a God-_____ life. Explain what each of these means, especially in the insanity we might conclude to life.

10. What does Psalm 34:11 tell us about the fear of God? How is Ecclesiastes a lesson plan for that purpose? How does the rest of Psalm 34 lead us to a fear of God? How does Psalm 36:1-2 speak to the fear of God in the face of the folly of Vanity Fair?

And Abram said, 'Behold, you have given me no offspring,
and a member of my household will be my heir.'
And behold, the word of the LORD came to him:
'This man shall not be your heir; your very own son shall
be your heir.' And he brought him outside and said,
'Look towards heaven, and number the stars, if you are
able to number them.' Then he said to him,
'So shall your offspring be.'
… Now Sarai, Abram's wife, had borne him no children.
She had a female Egyptian servant whose name was
Hagar. And Sarai said to Abram, 'Behold now, the LORD
has prevented me from bearing children. Go in to my
servant; it may be that I shall obtain children by her.'
And Abram listened to the voice of Sarai

(Genesis 15:3-5; 16:1-2).

3.
Vanity of planning and organization

The key to understanding the book of Ecclesiastes is to see its goal and how it achieves that goal. The goal is stated in the last two verses of the book (Eccles. 12:13-14), summarized as 'Fear God and keep his commandments.' How the book takes us there is by way of two teachers. As we have noted, the first teacher (called 'the Preacher') is a religious observer to life. He looks at life 'under the sun' and concludes life is 'vanity' (empty, meaningless, pointless), a chasing after wind. Good people die. Bad people prosper. The second teacher (unnamed), whose comments bracket those of the first teacher in Ecclesiastes 1:1-11 and 12:8-14, affirms what the Preacher says but insists that there is more to it than meets the eye. He lifts us to a vantage point above the sun, beyond the fallen created order, to a God who is and who reigns.

Now we begin to explore the various vanities spread across the spectrum of life, and we learn to use the interpretive key given to us by God.

Order

In his collection of observations under the sun, the Preacher notices a rhythm to life, some sort of order that includes good times and bad, ordinary and extraordinary.

> For everything there is a season, and a time for every matter under heaven:
>
> a time to be born, and a time to die;
> a time to plant, and a time to pluck up what is planted;
> a time to kill, and a time to heal;
> a time to break down, and a time to build up;
> a time to weep, and a time to laugh;
> a time to mourn, and a time to dance;
> a time to cast away stones, and a time to gather stones together;
> a time to embrace, and a time to refrain from embracing;
> a time to seek, and a time to lose;
> a time to keep, and a time to cast away;
> a time to tear, and a time to sew;
> a time to keep silence, and a time to speak;
> a time to love, and a time to hate;
> a time for war, and a time for peace.

> What gain has the worker from his toil? I have seen the business that God has given to the children of man to be busy with. He has made everything beautiful in its time. Also, he has put eternity into man's heart, yet so that he cannot find out what God has done from the beginning to the end. I perceived that there is nothing better for them than to be joyful and to do good as long as they live; also that everyone should eat and drink and take pleasure in all his toil — this is God's gift to man
> (Eccles. 3:1-13).

Many of you will read the opening words of this passage to the tune of a 1960s song written by Pete Seeger for The Byrds entitled, 'Turn! Turn! Turn!' (or, 'To Everything There is a Season'). The entire song is based on Ecclesiastes 3:1-8 and represents the seasons of life that we all experience.

In his observations on life under the sun the Preacher takes note of several things in this series of seasons. He discovers order to life, a place for everything and everything in its place. He perceives the hand of God that gives life its structure. We rejoice in that with the change of seasons. We sing: 'summer and winter and springtime and harvest' in celebration of God's unchanging faithfulness. There is no shadow of turning with him. There's great comfort in that.

With the turn of summer into autumn, we know what to expect. So we pull out the jackets, get the rakes ready and buy the school supplies. We also prepare ourselves for the seasons of life. Young people in the work force in the USA set aside money in their 401K savings account, but those in retirement are more troubled by recent events in the economy as they have entered a season of life where those funds are drawn on and relied upon. We see orderliness in the seasons, but we don't know what those seasons may hold. The Preacher observes this as well and feels the futility and frustration of it.

What gain has the worker from his toil? I have seen the business that God has given to the children of man to be busy with. He has made everything beautiful in its time. Also, he has put eternity into man's heart, yet so that he cannot find out what God has done from the beginning to the end

(3:9-11).

When I applied my heart to know wisdom, and to see the business that is done on earth, how neither day nor night do one's eyes see sleep, then I saw all the work of

God, that man cannot find out the work that is done under the sun. However much man may toil in seeking, he will not find it out. Even though a wise man claims to know, he cannot find it out

(8:16-17).

As a religious observer to life, the Preacher tries to dust for the fingerprints of God, seeing evidence of order but frustrated in finding rhyme or reason to what happens under the sun. He knows God is there somewhere, but glaring is man's inability to figure it out, let alone exercise any measure of control.

The question for us as we apply the interpretive key we have identified is: how does the perspective above the sun that knows and trusts and walks with God transform this uncertainty and frustration? Ecclesiastes speaks to this in three ways related to control.

Efforts to control

All of us try to find some measure of control in our lives. We buy insurance to cover us in the unexpected eventualities of accidents and the expected eventuality of death. We beat back the advancing weeds during the summer, providing ourselves with a haven from the ever-advancing forces of nature. We make plans and we make wills and do all sorts of things to maintain some control on life and to prepare for tomorrow.

The Preacher observes people working hard and planning wisely only to have their best-laid plans frustrated.

So I hated life, because what is done under the sun was grievous to me, for all is vanity and a striving after wind.

Vanity of planning and organization

I hated all my toil in which I toil under the sun, seeing that I must leave it to the man who will come after me, and who knows whether he will be wise or a fool? Yet he will be master of all for which I toiled and used my wisdom under the sun. This also is vanity. So I turned about and gave my heart up to despair over all the toil of my labours under the sun, because sometimes a person who has toiled with wisdom and knowledge and skill must leave everything to be enjoyed by someone who did not toil for it. This also is vanity and a great evil

(2:17-21).

We can relate to that. So we all try to find some stability, some degree of control through our careful planning and organization. When we raise our children we try our very best to control what they are exposed to and influenced by, to keep them from going astray and lead them in the right way. We have family devotions and teach them the Bible and make sure they are in church. We guard their education to try to control what they learn. But many of us can attest that our best efforts are no guarantee that they will be walking with Christ.

We try to find control through politics. In GOP (America's Republican 'Grand Old Party'), we trust. But politicians disappoint and even the best laws enacted fail to protect our interests or promote our values. It seems so futile.

We organize our days as best we can, but our planning is written on the shoreline ready for the waves to wash away. A friend of mine spent time carefully organizing his day, filling it with all sorts of things he wanted to accomplish, mapping it all out according to a carefully constructed schedule. Ready to get things underway, he went out to his car and before he got to his first planned event the water pump on his car broke and he had to call a tow truck. Then, almost as if to reinforce the point, he left his planning calendar with all its carefully constructed information in the car at the place where the car had been towed. So it goes.

We buy insurance to provide for us in need, only to discover our policy does not cover the flooding caused by the hurricane. We are careful to protect our safety, buckling our seatbelts, looking before crossing the street, yet the unexpected exposes the futility of our best laid plans. Sometimes it works. Sometimes it doesn't. We try to eat right and keep fit so that we stay healthy, but disease and injury thwart those efforts.

We do make efforts to control, to manage life — and we should. God calls us to. He gives us permission to plan. God calls us to be responsible stewards of all that we have mentioned. But if we are honest with ourselves we realize how futile are our efforts and illusory is the measure of control we think we have. We can all identify with the Preacher's observations that seem to align more with Murphy's Law than God's.

Effects of lack of control

How do you think my friend felt when his best-laid plans imploded before they even got started? When we put our hope in our plans to try to find certainty and stability under the sun, what effect does it have on our lives? The Preacher says we find anxiety and pain and grief.

The Preacher felt despair, a profound sense of helplessness and even a 'Why bother?' attitude, akin to striving after wind. Listen to the voice he gives to the vanity he tries to make sense of.

What has a man from all the toil and striving of heart with which he toils beneath the sun? For all his days are full of sorrow, and his work is a vexation. Even in the night his heart does not rest. This also is vanity

(2:22-23).

For there is a time and a way for everything, although man's trouble lies heavy on him. For he does not know what is to be, for who can tell him how it will be? No man has power to retain the spirit, or power over the day of death. There is no discharge from war, nor will wickedness deliver those who are given to it. All this I observed while applying my heart to all that is done under the sun, when man had power over man to his hurt

(8:6-9).

Realizing we can't control, we plunge into worry, often right into the deep end. Worry is the by-product of our effort of control under the sun. Instead of fearing God, recognizing and embracing our limitations and deferring to him, worry grasps for the prerogative of God. Worry wants control. It wants knowledge of the 'what will happen'. It wants power over the 'what ifs'. We don't want to relinquish control because we want our will to be done. So we find ourselves even resisting God, not trusting that he will do what we want or what we think best. And who's to blame us? After all, if we as parents protect our children to the best of our ability, shouldn't God as our Father protect us and do what is best for us as his children according to his ability? But will he, we question, as we seek to take the reins from his hand?

The effects of our inability to control can wash over us as panic, worry, fear, anger, grief and despair, sometimes all mixed together in depression. These symptoms of not fearing God can govern our lives and they can be a foothold for Satan to turn us against God.

Our Lord Jesus, as the Great Physician, gives us an anatomy lesson on worry in his Sermon on the Mount in Matthew 6, where he exposes worry as the condition of seeking our kingdom over the kingdom of our God, laying up treasures on earth rather than in heaven, trying to pry the things of tomorrow from the hand of our God rather than living in his provision for the day. Jesus makes it clear that the antidote to worry, peace instead of panic, is achieved not by supplanting God but by submitting ourselves, our wills and our goals to him.

Effective control

The Preacher makes his observations under the sun, but how is that perspective redeemed and transformed by the unnamed teacher as he bids us to fear God and to keep his commandments?

The foundation stone to put in place as a matter of first importance is this: only God controls. Only God has a right to control. Fearing God is acknowledging and embracing both the prerogative of God to govern all things for his purposes that are hidden to us, and submitting our lives and desires to him. Fearing God is giving him the place of control, recognizing we don't have it in the first place. Obeying his commands looks to trust and obey him in whatever he brings to us, entrusting ourselves to our faithful Creator and continuing to do good. It is to say that only God controls and that knowledge will bring delight and will direct how I think and act.

Through his prophet, God challenges us when we allow the perspective under the sun to form conclusions about life or about God, even supposing he does not know or does not care. Through his prophets, God puts words to this effect in our mouths:

Why do you say, O Jacob, and speak, O Israel, 'My way is hidden from the LORD, and my right is disregarded by my God'? Have you not known? Have you not heard? The LORD is the everlasting God, the Creator of the ends of the earth. He does not faint or grow weary; his understanding is unsearchable. He gives power to the faint, and to him who has no might he increases strength. Even youths shall faint and be weary, and young men shall fall exhausted; but they who wait for the LORD shall renew their strength; they shall mount up with wings like eagles; they shall run and not be weary; they shall walk and not faint

(Isaiah 40:27-31).

We look under the sun. We grimace at the pain and uncertainty in our lives. We match up our experience with what we want to think about God. And we conclude that either God is not sovereign, or he is not good, or he is just plain oblivious. We say, 'My way is hidden from the Lord' (i.e., God doesn't know) or we say, 'My right is disregarded by my God' (i.e., God doesn't care).

That's the perspective under the sun. God gives the same answer he gave to Job when his foundation crumbled around him. God recites his divine résumé for Job. Who made all that is? Did you? Who controls all these things? Do you? Job's response is to cover his mouth with his hand to keep him from challenging and charging God.

And then Job says this:

Then Job answered the LORD and said: 'I know that you can do all things, and that no purpose of yours can be thwarted. "Who is this that hides counsel without knowledge?" Therefore I have uttered what I did not understand, things too wonderful for me, which I did not know. "Hear, and I will speak; I will question you, and you make it known to me." I had heard of you by the hearing of the ear, but now my eye sees you; therefore I despise myself, and repent in dust and ashes'

(Job 42:1-6).

That 'seeing God' is what Ecclesiastes calls 'fearing God', as it breaks through the 'under the sun' barrier. It is to see God as God and give him the glory, the right. God has the role of control and the right of control. If I live, I live for Christ. If I die, I die for Christ. My hope is in God. Though he slay me, yet will I praise him.

To fear God and to keep his commandments gives us a perspective above the sun and leads us to appreciate the order God gives to a fallen world ravaged by the effects of sin, and in hard times to submit to him, to trust in him, to seek him, to loosen our grip and to cast our cares upon him, to hope in his answer to the futility of this world, Jesus Christ, who assures us we will have trouble in this world, but to take heart, because he has overcome the world. Fearing God takes to heart Jesus' counsel in the Sermon on the Mount:

But seek first the kingdom of God and his righteousness, and all these things will be added to you. Therefore do not be anxious about tomorrow, for tomorrow will be anxious for itself. Sufficient for the day is its own trouble

(Matthew 6:33-34).

While out driving on the road I found myself behind a car displaying a bumper sticker that read, 'Life Can Be Beautiful — One Day at a Time'. That pithy prescription became parabolic for our Lord's approach to worry as the car to which the bumper sticker was affixed was dangling from a tow truck. Challenge by challenge, in the expected and unexpected, God's grace is sufficient for the day. As with his dispensation of manna, he wants us to live one day at a time, neither grasping for knowledge of the future nor bucking against the constraints of our created humanity. Instead, fear of God and obedience to his commandments engender a childlike contentment in God's providence and trust in his provision.

Does that mean we don't plan in this life under the sun? Does that mean we don't guard our children's education, or that we shouldn't care whom we vote for? It doesn't mean that, but fearing God and keeping his commands mean that our hope is in God and our plans are written in pencil. As James counsels us:

Come now, you who say, 'Today or tomorrow we will go into such and such a town and spend a year there and trade and make a profit'— yet you do not know what tomorrow will bring. What is your life? For you are a mist that appears for a little time and then vanishes. Instead you ought to say, 'If the Lord wills, we will live and do this or that.' As it is, you boast in your arrogance. All such boasting is evil

(James 4:13-16).

The Byrds' 'Turn, Turn, Turn' was immensely popular. Not only did it speak to an orderliness and rhythm, it suggested a sort of hope. Yes, there is a time to mourn, but hang in there, because a time to dance is coming.

The entire text of the song is adapted from Ecclesiastes 3:1-8, except for one phrase added by Pete Seeger. That addition is found at the very end of the song. It goes like this:

To everything (turn, turn, turn)
There is a season (turn, turn, turn)
And a time for every purpose, under heaven

Making sanity out of vanity

A time to gain, a time to lose
A time to rend, a time to sew
A time to love, a time to hate
A time for peace, *I swear it's not too late.*

In the tumultuous 1960s that saw America's involvement in the Vietnam War, 'Turn, Turn, Turn' was a plea for peace. It was a call for people to do something to end the war, end the hate — for man to break into this time for every purpose under heaven, to find some measure of control, to restore some semblance of order.

True, people can be peacemakers, but the peace Pete Seeger longed for is a peace found only in Jesus Christ. He is the sure and unshakable foundation. He is the end of personal animosity and national conflict. In him are found peace with God and the peace of God. And so as redemptive realists we lift our eyes to him who holds the times in his hand and we find peace and joy and hope as pilgrims living under the sun, longing for the life to come.

Questions from Qoheleth

1. How does the Preacher express the rhythm he sees to life? What comfort do we derive from that rhythm?
2. What does it mean that God has put eternity into man's heart in Ecclesiastes 3:11a? How does the observation that follows in Ecclesiastes 3:11b highlight the Preacher's conflict and set the stage for the perspective of the unnamed teacher?
3. What are some examples of our efforts to find some measure of control in managing life under the sun? How can our attempts at control act contrary to the fear of God and actually bring us to oppose God?

4. How is worry a symptom of the heart problem of not fearing God? How do the following passages address worry in keeping with a call to fear God in respect to life's uncertainties? How would each guide Abraham and Sarah in Genesis 15 and 16?
   a. Isaiah 40:27-31
   b. Matt. 6:19-34
   c. Phil. 4:4-10

5. What are you worried about right now? How are you resisting God rather than resting in him? What does the contrast of Matthew 6:19-21 and Matthew 6:33 suggest is the real issue of your worry? In keeping with Matthew 6:34, what about your situation can you put in the 'today' category for action and put in the 'tomorrow' category for direction? How does the manna metaphor apply to both the today and tomorrow categories?

6. How does thanksgiving in Philippians 4:6 take the wind out of worry? For what are we to give thanks in the face of worry?

7. Does God prohibit planning and organization? How does he regulate it according to James 4:13-16?

8. How does worry belong more to the Preacher's vantage point than to the unnamed teacher's? What does faith introduce to this vantage point? See Isaiah 41:9-10.

9. How does The Lord's Prayer in Matthew 6:9-13 give voice to Jesus' concern in Matthew 6:19-34? What should be prayer's agenda in dealing with worry?

A man of many companions may come to ruin,
but there is a friend who sticks closer than a brother
(Proverbs 18:24).

4.

Vanity of family and friends

We held a missions conference at my church, inviting several missionaries from different parts of the world to update us on their work, and to encourage them in their difficult calling. During a discussion with one of the missionaries I mentioned that I was preaching a series on Ecclesiastes. When she heard that, one of those wry grins crossed her face, she just shook her head, and said what a hard book it is to make head or tail of. It seems so negative. Her reaction suggested that it was one of the least likely books for a sermon series. It's hard to disagree with her.

We've seen that the bulk of Ecclesiastes contains the ponderings of a religious observer to life, someone called 'the Preacher'. This Preacher speaks in the first person ('I'). He is called the 'Preacher', not in the sense of one expositing the Word of God, but more as a collector and conveyor of thoughts on life. The perspective from which he makes his observations is 'under the sun' and what he sees is not very encouraging. The good die young. The wicked prosper. So he concludes that all is vanity, meaningless, pointless. His advice seems to boil down to us just having to try to make the most of things, to enjoy what we can and hope for the best.

We've also noted that the religious ponderings of the Preacher are framed by another teacher, one not named. He speaks in the third person about what the Preacher has said, except that his perspective looks beyond 'under the sun', beyond the fallen created order. He affirms the Preacher's observations, but he insists on a radically different perspective and encourages a posture of faith. His counsel is to fear God and keep his commandments. And this counsel touches on and transforms every aspect of life the Preacher surveys.

In the previous chapter we began to inventory these aspects of life, looking at the vanity of planning and organization — our best efforts to gain some measure of control over life. But fearing God, we are to defer to his will and trust in his perfect providence as we hand the reins of life over to him. In the model of our Lord Jesus, we are to say, 'Not my will but your will be done,' in whatever cup our Father might set before us.

In this chapter, we turn to another category from the Preacher's collection of observations under the sun where we try to find meaning or in which we immerse ourselves to try to find escape from the harsh realities of life — relationships. We cannot help but nod in agreement at the Preacher's conflicted observations and assessments on the subject.

As a pastor, I have sat down countless times with people whose lives have come crashing down upon them because of a broken relationship. A wife has left her husband and the husband is crushed. He says, 'She's my life. I don't know how I can go on.' A teenager has rebelled and left home, and the parents are desperate, at their wits' end, plunged into palpable despair. A single woman is frantic with fear that she'll never be able to find a husband. She cannot see herself at peace until she's married with children.

Relationships are as much a staple of life as bread and water, part of God's design for society and for us as social beings. We've got family, friends, co-workers. At the same time, relationships are a source of pain, anxiety and frustration. We can look at what God tells us about relationships in Ecclesiastes under three headings.

Riches of relationships

Relationships are a blessing. The proverb says, 'He who finds a wife finds a good thing, and obtains favour from the Lord.' My wife, Linda, and I have been married for thirty-five years, and I can confirm that in her I have found a good thing and obtained favour from the Lord. God used Linda to lead me to Christ. I had a religious background but did not know what it was to be a Christian until I met her and saw her life in religious practice that flowed from the inside out. She's the one who introduced me to sound Bible teaching.

We have four children. As Pastor Dad, I've had the privilege to marry my daughter, Sarah, to Joe; and my son, Luke, to Lindsay. Grandchildren have come along, five and counting, and they are a joy. After some lengthy debates (twenty-one months' worth), we just settled on 'Pop Pop' as my *nom de grandpater*. My choice, 'GrandStan', was dismissed as disrespectful and unpronounceable. Relationships are good. They are blessings from the God who designed us as social beings. Relationships enrich our lives. We are better for them.

The Preacher in Ecclesiastes sees the great benefits of relationship.

> Two are better than one, because they have a good reward for their toil. For if they fall, one will lift up his fellow. But woe to him who is alone when he falls and has not another to lift him up! Again, if two lie together, they keep warm, but how can one keep warm alone? And though a man might prevail against one who

is alone, two will withstand him — a threefold cord is
not quickly broken

(4:9-12).

We all can relate to the blessings of others in our lives, not
only them to us but us to them. The Preacher notes four areas
where we benefit from others: work, woe, warmth and war.
Take each of these areas and remove the other person and feel
how much more difficult things are. God has made us social
beings and given us relationships to enrich our lives. Although
God's design for relationships is prominent before the Fall,
that design continues in a new wrinkle to help sustain one
another on this side of the Fall under the sun. A friend stands
by us in time of trial or works beside us to fend off the ever-
advancing weeds that encroach upon us in this world beset by
the ravages of sin.

The Preacher observes how shallow and empty life is
without significant others in his life:

Again, I saw vanity under the sun: one person who has
no other, either son or brother, yet there is no end to all
his toil, and his eyes are never satisfied with riches, so
that he never asks, 'For whom am I toiling and depriving
myself of pleasure?' This also is vanity and an unhappy
business

(4:7-8).

I had a difficult childhood. I can vouch for the value of
relationships over money. I lived with a drunken grandmother
and for a period of time basically raised myself. I had no
friends. I remember in elementary school pulling out a wad
of cash and buying things from the cafeteria for classmates
with the misdirected idea that they would then like me. The
Preacher observes how unsatisfying riches are without another

to share them with, because the greater riches are found in the relationships of our lives.

Reliability of relationships

Yet with relationships come headaches and heartaches. Single people are sometimes gripped with fear that they won't find someone to marry. The relationships we count on let us down. To use the example of the Preacher, when we fall the person we counted on to be there to pick us up in our woe is not there. That can hurt — deeply. Marriage partners, who pledged their troth till death do them part, turn their spouse in for a newer model. The person before whom you could be naked in every sense of the word — vulnerable, exposed, real, warts and all — turns his back on you in violation of his commitment to you of the steadfast inviolability of your bond. That cuts deep. With no perforated line to neatly sever the marriage bond when it is ripped apart, divorce hurts and scars and prompts insecurity and fear. The same is true to a degree of friendships. Who of us has not been betrayed?

The Preacher in Ecclesiastes sees how fickle and futile relationships can be under the sun. Why bother? People are just going to let you down. How many pastors have sat before a couple madly in love, committed to Christ, leading them in biblical preparation for a marriage that has all the markings of a thing of beauty. Five years later, that couple who were so in love cannot stand each other. Is an enduring marriage, a stable friendship, just striving after wind? Just the other day, someone asked me the secret to the love and mutual enjoyment of my marriage, because she has observed the preponderance of marriages as failed, if not in divorce then in ruptured relationship, with husband and wife at best as housemates, at worst cohabitating belligerents.

Sometimes the failure of relationships is not even either person's fault. My life was radically changed one day in first grade. My mother was on her way to collect me from school. She never made it. She was killed when a pick-up truck drove through a 'Stop' sign and slammed into her car. My brother, Michael, was in the back seat. I never saw them again. Death is the ultimate severer of relationships. The Preacher takes note of that. Your mum, your siblings — you count on those relationships, you take them for granted. But you look under the sun and realize the risk of counting on them. Some, after being burnt by a broken relationship, refuse to open themselves again to the pain of being rejected. They live jaded with the cynicism of the Preacher. The saying, 'It is better to have loved and lost than never to have loved at all,' is lost on them. For the time, they can find no redeeming value in intimacy. Often, they look elsewhere, immersing themselves in work or another of the offerings of Vanity Fair.

The conclusion of the Preacher is that companionship is a good thing, given by God, but it's likely to disappoint and leave you hurt and alone. How did he put it? 'This also is vanity and an unhappy business.'

Redemptive relationships

The unnamed teacher tells his son, 'The Preacher is right. People let you down. You'll let people down. If you invest your fulfilment and your hope and your stability in relationships, you're in for a letdown. Not only may they crumble beneath you, even if they don't, they can't give you what you're expecting of them.' His counsel to deal with life under the sun, coping with the created order fallen under the ravages of sin, is to 'fear God and keep his commandments'.

How does fearing God and keeping his commandments transform life for us under the sun? The Preacher in Ecclesiastes forces us to be realists, but the unnamed teacher and the purpose of the book is to make us redemptive realists, living in the light of the gospel. How does a worldview that gives God his due and seeks to honour him redemptively regulate and revolutionize our relationships?

When that woman asked me the secret to the love and mutual enjoyment of my marriage, in view of the listless and loveless and even internecine marriages she has observed, my answer to her was Linda's and my mutual commitment first to Christ and from that to one another. I've shared with those I've counselled how the first year of my marriage was rocky. My guess is that if Linda and I had not been believers, our marriage would have dissolved. What kept us together and committed to working through things was the backbone of our obedience to Christ related to the permanence of the marriage relationship as he taught. But that obedience proved as Kevlar, the stuff of which they make bulletproof vests. And by the grace of God, we persevered and flourished, for which I am thankful.

You see what surfaced in the conflict of our 'honeymoon year', what asserted itself as governor of our hearts and home? We weren't left with just self. Fear of God and obedience to his commandments figured prominently and took our marriage in a direction of which the navigation system under the sun is incapable. To God be the glory!

Fearing God will drive you into the arms of the God of glory who has taken you as his very own, and those arms will hold you in the love he has lavished upon you in Jesus Christ. Listen to what your God tells you to encourage you and sustain you in your days under the sun.

You whom I took from the ends of the earth, and called from its farthest corners, saying to you, 'You are my servant, I have chosen you and not cast you off'; fear not, for I am with you; be not dismayed, for I am your God; I will strengthen you, I will help you, I will uphold you with my righteous right hand

(Isaiah 41:9-10).

But now thus says the LORD, he who created you, O Jacob, he who formed you, O Israel: 'Fear not, for I have redeemed you; I have called you by name, you are mine. When you pass through the waters, I will be with you; and through the rivers, they shall not overwhelm you; when you walk through fire you shall not be burned, and the flame shall not consume you. For I am the LORD your God, the Holy One of Israel, your Saviour. I give Egypt as your ransom, Cush and Seba in exchange for you. Because you are precious in my eyes, and honoured, and I love you, I give men in return for you, peoples in exchange for your life. Fear not, for I am with you; I will bring your offspring from the east, and from the west I will gather you

(Isaiah 43:1-5).

Our God speaks to us in the midst of our troubles with words of grace and care to comfort us with his presence, to assure us of his love, to let us know that, while others may leave or forsake us, he will not. In the Isaiah 41 passage, the promises of God's presence, protection and provision are not indiscriminate. They are wrapped in grace and given to those on whom God has set his love, whom he has called to himself from the ends of the earth.

That love for us is realized in Jesus Christ, from eternity past.

Blessed be the God and Father of our Lord Jesus Christ, who has blessed us in Christ with every spiritual blessing in the heavenly places, even as he chose us in him before the foundation of the world, that we should be holy and blameless before him. In love he predestined us for adoption through Jesus Christ, according to the purpose of his will, to the praise of his glorious grace, with which he has blessed us in the Beloved

(Ephesians 1:3-6).

God pledged his troth, his steadfast, loyal, relentless, unwavering love to you, and that love will not let you go. God set his love on you while you were an outcast who reviled him and rebelled against him. God came to you as an orphan to adopt you as his very own. God fills his Word with metaphors of relationship to convince you of his love that will abide though others may let you down.

As a believer, you live in reconciled relationship with God and nothing can separate you from that love. When my mother and brother were killed in that car accident, my life would never be the same. Though I found a roof over my head and some measure of love in each situation, I felt like a baton passed from one location to the next, a necessary burden that was part of the familial race duty-bound to continue, rain or shine. Yet in retrospect I see the hand of God leading, caring for, providing for, preparing me for the plans he had for me, eventually leading me to a relationship with him and a love that transcends anything under the sun could offer and calling me to minister to others with the comfort I had received. God will never let you go. He will never leave you nor forsake you. You can count on his abiding love in Jesus Christ. You will never lack the embrace of his everlasting arms. Not even death itself will be able to separate you from his love for you in Christ Jesus.

As for those relationships under the sun, giving God the fear due his name will transform those relationships with others, as you seek to love as you have been loved and to love as you are loved by God, a love grounded in mercy and grace. Certainly, you don't want to put your relationships with family and friends in the place of God, but neither do you want to minimize the value of those relationships. You will be able to love those who hurt you, loving your neighbour and even your enemy, exercising protective love, proactive love.

Love in the Bible can be commanded and is commanded. The two great commandments as summaries of the law are to love God with all your being and to love your neighbour as yourself, in whatever relationship you may have with that neighbour. You won't find a theoretical definition of love in the Bible. Rather, you will find it operationally defined. Revisit the classic passage on love from 1 Corinthians 13:4-7. Observe the 'how to' of loving your enemy from Luke 6:27-26. Notice the illustrations of love that God holds up for us in John 3:16 and 1 John 3:16. The common denominator involves doing: it is functional rather than theoretical love.

By fearing God and keeping his commandments, you will be able to enjoy the relationships of family and friends as gifts of God, in which you can honour God. You will not be surprised by betrayal and, while the pain will be real and cut deep, you will find comfort and security and strength in that love that will not let you go.

Unmasking idolatry

We see now what we're really talking about when we speak of the vanity of family and friends, the vanity of strength and beauty and all those other vanities we'll explore from the Preacher's observations. We're talking about idolatry. The unnamed teacher leads us through the mall of Vanity Fair, stopping by each kiosk of the world's offerings under the sun to explain how it can only disappoint in and of itself. It will never satisfy. Rather, fear God — trust in him, delight yourself in him. Don't substitute a husband, a wife, a son, a daughter, a friend, a mentor, a hero, anyone... for God. Obey his commands, starting with the command to love and all that that entails — as far as it concerns you, be at peace with all men. Bring the gospel to reform yourself through the love of Christ and to transform the relationships of your life under the sun.

In a nutshell, savour the love of family and friends, but trust only in the love of God in Christ. As the proverb says: 'A man of many companions may come to ruin, but there is a friend who sticks closer than a brother' (Prov. 18:24) — that friend is the one who loves you to death.

Questions from Qoheleth

1. What blessings does the Preacher mention in Ecclesiastes 4:9-12? How does each of these blessings benefit us that being alone would not?
2. Read Genesis 2:18. Why would God conclude that it was 'not good' that man should be alone? What practical issue of being alone relates to Genesis 1:27-28? What are some issues other than this practical one that relate to God's design for relationship?
3. What are some benefits of friendship? How can you tell someone is a friend?
4. What risk is involved in intimate friendship? Marriage is the most intimate of human relationships, involving the greatest degree of openness and vulnerability, but friendship finds itself on this scale as well. How might Genesis 2:25 apply to marriage? To friendship?

5. How does life under the sun negatively impact relationships? How do relationships help us under the sun?
6. In what way can a relationship become a chasing after wind? How have you seen this illustrated in your experience?
7. How does fearing God restore a proper perspective to relationships? How does it regulate relationships?
8. What do redemptive relationships look like according to passages like Colossians 3:12-17?
9. How does a relationship with God differ from human relationships? In what way is this relationship with him foundational to healthy human relationships?
10. How does our relationship with God lead us to act redemptively relative to those who may not be responsive or may not reciprocate? See Romans 12:14-21.

Why should I fear in times of trouble,
when the iniquity of those who cheat me
surrounds me,
those who trust in their wealth
and boast of the abundance of their riches?
Truly no man can ransom another,
or give to God the price of his life,
for the ransom of their life is costly
and can never suffice,
that he should live on for ever
and never see the pit
(Psalm 49:5-9).

5.

Vanity of financial security and possessions

Two voices and two vantage points provide the structure for understanding the book of Ecclesiastes. The voice of the Preacher coming to us in the first person chronicles life under the sun and the picture we find is a frustrating and unsettling one. Another voice, this in the third person, touches on and transforms all the Preacher's observations by lifting us to the vantage point of faith to see the God who is and who reigns over all. This unnamed voice calls upon us to fear God and obey him, giving us the bearings of wisdom as we navigate our way through a vexing existence.

By bringing the God-centred, God-serving perspective and protocol of the unnamed teacher to the futility of the Preacher's religious survey, the senselessness we observe in life becomes tethered to the plan and purposes of a sovereign God. The angst and futility that we experience are replaced with hope and meaning.

We've seen this with relationships where those closest to us can let us down. We can and do let them down too. But relationships, even the closest of relationships, that of husband and wife, cannot be a substitute for God. We cannot make an idol out of family. Those relationships, however, are redeemed as we glorify God in them according to the counsel of his revealed will.

In this chapter we turn the page in the Preacher's journal of observations under the sun to another area where we try to find stability, significance and escape in life — money and possessions.

How quickly things change. It wasn't so long ago that the value of my home reached a level I could not have imagined, spurred on by the rising real estate market. My retirement funds had grown modestly but steadily over the years of my working life. Then the bottom dropped out. The stock market plummeted, taking along with it the value of just about everything.

Just when it seemed the stock market could not go lower, the Dow Jones index dropped by another round of triple digit losses. Then the federal government came to the rescue. The 700-plus billion dollar relief plan passed through Congress. Still the market dropped. The government cut the interest rate. Still the market dropped. The president promised to shore up banks. Yet nothing made any difference as fear increased and confidence drained out of investors. Like a dropped spool of thread, the market continued its freefall and with it unravelled the security of those once brimming with untouchable swagger.

Many of the financial institutions that used to be mainstays of the American economy have crumbled like sandcastles pulled down by the outgoing tide. Our personal investments and retirement accounts have been leaking like a punctured water balloon. From inflated prices to deflated spirits — who could see it all coming?

Financial futility is no surprise for the Preacher in the book of Ecclesiastes. He observes people under the sun working all their lives with nothing to show for it. Hard work is supposed to translate into financial stability — but there's no guarantee. He sees others getting what we work hard for. All that we have accumulated can disappear in an instant — and with it the confidence and hope we had tied to it.

In this anchor store of the mall of Vanity Fair, Ecclesiastes leads us through the well-stocked aisles, where savings are realized by how much something is discounted ('I saved 30 per cent!'), but where the wind is quickly taken out of our 'sales'. The Preacher notes the futility of it all but the unnamed teacher interjects to tout redemption in relationship with God, who, as opposed to the bank that changes its name with the latest takeover, is the same yesterday, today and for ever. We can touch on three aspects of the spreadsheet of sanity in the midst of the vanity of a fickle financial world.

Credits — the value of material assets

Our God has blessed us abundantly. He has opened his hand and supplied our needs. He has filled our lives with good things. Take inventory of all that you have: your car, your home, your computer, your stuff — all these things are from God. As Paul puts it, 'What do you have that you did not receive?' (1 Cor. 4:7).

When we sit down to a meal, what do we do? We give thanks to our God for his provision. Our labours may have paid for it and our efforts prepared the meal, but it's all from God who gives us ability and opportunity.

Money and possessions are good and necessary, and provide enjoyment in life. The Preacher takes such note in his religious observations.

> There is nothing better for a person than that he should eat and drink and find enjoyment in his toil. This also, I saw, is from the hand of God, for apart from him who can eat or who can have enjoyment?
>
> (Eccles. 2:24-25).

The Preacher also observes that wisdom and money carry similar benefit.

> For the protection of wisdom is like the protection of money, and the advantage of knowledge is that wisdom preserves the life of him who has it
>
> (Eccles. 7:12).

Money does provide protection, as anyone whose car breaks down and has the resources in the bank to get it fixed can attest. We save for these very things.

The Preacher suggests that our finances do meet our needs and grant us some measure of security and protection. It's comforting to have a cushion. In other words, there is great value to material assets as gifts of God, given for our enjoyment.

Debits — the vapour of material assets

The problem, though, is when money and material possessions take on an improper place in our lives, our hopes, our dreams, our ambitions, our security. Jesus makes this clear in his response to a question about money matters.

> Someone in the crowd said to him, 'Teacher, tell my brother to divide the inheritance with me.' But he said to him, 'Man, who made me a judge or arbitrator over you?' And he said to them, 'Take care, and be on your guard against all covetousness, for one's life does not consist in the abundance of one's possessions.' And he told them a parable, saying, 'The land of a rich man produced plentifully, and he thought to himself, "What

shall I do, for I have nowhere to store my crops?" And he said, "I will do this: I will tear down my barns and build larger ones, and there I will store all my grain and my goods. And I will say to my soul, Soul, you have ample goods laid up for many years; relax, eat, drink, be merry." But God said to him, "Fool! This night your soul is required of you, and the things you have prepared, whose will they be?" So is the one who lays up treasure for himself and is not rich toward God'

(Luke 12:13-21).

Jesus points out the foolishness of relying on financial security and the emptiness of defining life in terms of material possessions. His parable carries with it echoes of the book of Ecclesiastes. Notice the parallel reasoning between the rich man of Jesus' parable and the Preacher.

'"And I will say to my soul, Soul, you have ample goods laid up for many years; relax, eat, drink, be merry." But God said to him, "Fool! This night your soul is required of you, and the things you have prepared, whose will they be?"'

(Luke 12:19-20).

So I turned about and gave my heart up to despair over all the toil of my labours under the sun, because sometimes a person who has toiled with wisdom and knowledge and skill must leave everything to be enjoyed by someone who did not toil for it. This also is vanity and a great evil ... There is nothing better for a person than that he should eat and drink and find enjoyment in his toil. This also, I saw, is from the hand of God

(Eccles. 2:20-21,24).

Making sanity out of vanity

What Jesus is saying is that material assets can never take the place of God as our hope, an ever-present help in trouble that we should not fear, our shelter in time of storm. In that way the current financial crisis serves as a modern-day parable from the God whose providence governs all that comes to pass.

Money has a place but giving money the wrong place in our lives can rob us of peace, of hope, of real treasure. It can drive us by wrong motives.

> Then I saw that all toil and all skill in work come from a man's envy of his neighbour. This also is vanity and a striving after wind
>
> (Eccles. 4:4).

It can give us false hope, as the Preacher painfully notes.

> He who loves money will not be satisfied with money, nor he who loves wealth with his income; this also is vanity. When goods increase, they increase who eat them, and what advantage has their owner but to see them with his eyes? Sweet is the sleep of a labourer, whether he eats little or much, but the full stomach of the rich will not let him sleep.
>
> There is a grievous evil that I have seen under the sun: riches were kept by their owner to his hurt, and those riches were lost in a bad venture. And he is father of a son, but he has nothing in his hand. As he came from his mother's womb he shall go again, naked as he came, and shall take nothing for his toil that he may carry away in his hand. This also is a grievous evil: just as he came, so shall he go, and what gain is there to him who toils for the wind?
>
> (Eccles. 5:10-16)

Mishandling of money's motivation can even degenerate into what Malachi calls 'robbing God'. Pastor Mike Ross tells of a time when he was a pastoral intern at a church.

'The senior minister told me something that shocked me. Sitting in his office in our weekly meeting and talking about church finances, the pastor said to me, "Mike, there are at least six millionaires in this congregation, and you and Jane, on a seminarian's salary, give more to [this church] than any of them do." This was not intended as a compliment to me' (PCA, *50 Days of Prayer*, 2008).

Ross' comment speaks to the lack of a God-centredness that sees goods as given by God, to be used for him and investment in his kingdom. Tithing and generosity are not the issues in themselves. Rather, they are symptomatic of our focus and indicative of where we are concerned to invest. That's the danger of money and why Jesus spoke so often about it. It can occupy a place in our hearts and position in our lives that belong only to God. That's why it is an anchor store in the mall of Vanity Fair — because it attracts such traffic and is a major player in the struggle for true treasure.

Balance Sheet — the validity of material assets

The counsel of the unnamed teacher is to 'fear God and keep his commandments'. How does a fear of God and directing our lives by the teaching of his Word redeem our finances and material possessions?

Jesus' parable of the short-sighted fool who lived his life from the vantage point 'under the sun' and built bigger barns instructs us. We've heard the rebuke of Jesus upon the reasoning of the one who finds security in having and hoarding, looking to his 'ample goods' and living a life of self-indulgent leisure where he planned to 'relax, eat, drink and be merry'. Jesus introduces the fear of God who will say to him: 'Fool! This night your soul is required of you, and the things you have prepared, whose will they be?' Jesus' bottom line is this: 'So is the one who lays up treasure for himself and is not rich toward God.'

Here Jesus does just what the unnamed teacher does as he calls us to 'fear God and keep his commandments'. Jesus calls us to a God-invested life. What does it mean to be rich toward God? It means God is the desire of our heart, the apple of our eye. His glory, his kingdom are our ambition.

Jesus made this contrast and challenge for our lives abundantly clear in the Sermon on the Mount, as we were reminded earlier in respect to control. Money is one of those things in which we try to find control, but it also presents itself as a rival to God for our trust and allegiance. It can fuel worry when we see those things in which we trust being eroded, as we witness in today's volatile economy. To that Jesus says this:

> 'Therefore I tell you, do not be anxious about your life, what you will eat or what you will drink, nor about your body, what you will put on. Is not life more than food, and the body more than clothing?'
>
> (Matt. 6:25).

Then Jesus goes on to direct our eyes *under the sun* to God's care of the birds and the lilies. He chastises us:

> 'But if God so clothes the grass of the field, which today is alive and tomorrow is thrown into the oven, will he not much more clothe you, O you of little faith? Therefore do not be anxious, saying, "What shall we eat?" or "What shall we drink?" or "What shall we wear?" For the Gentiles seek after all these things, and your heavenly Father knows that you need them all'
>
> (Matt. 6:30-32).

Notice that Jesus gives us redemptive perspective as he speaks of God as 'Father' and contrasts Gentiles, who are without God and without hope in the world, with those who by God's grace count themselves children in relationship with their Heavenly Father.

Jesus calls us to fear God by trusting him and obeying him in the seeking of his kingdom as the overarching priority of our lives (Matt. 6:33), where moth and rust cannot destroy, and thieves cannot break in and steal. Trust in God affects daily provision and future investment. He lays out his plan for us in dealing with the uncertainty and instability of money and material goods:

'Therefore do not be anxious about tomorrow, for tomorrow will be anxious for itself. Sufficient for the day is its own trouble'

(Matt. 6:34).

The plan: consecrate the day to God in service; commit the next to God in trust.

The reason Jesus speaks about worry is not just to calm our fears. We've already seen that worry grasps for the prerogative of God in wanting control over the vicissitudes and variables of life (and valuables of life). Now we see that worry can be a red flag, a warning light in our Christian lives that we are more devoted to money than God, trusting for our security more in money than God. Worry as the guard dog to our treasure house seeks to find stability and contentment in the wrong place. The apostle Paul lays it on the line for us.

Now there is great gain in godliness with contentment, for we brought nothing into the world, and we cannot take anything out of the world. But if we have food and clothing, with these we will be content. But those who desire to be rich fall into temptation, into a snare, into many senseless and harmful desires that plunge people into ruin and destruction. For the love of money is a root of all kinds of evils. It is through this craving that some have wandered away from the faith and pierced themselves with many pangs...

As for the rich in this present age, charge them not to be haughty, nor to set their hopes on the uncertainty of riches, but on God, who richly provides us with everything to enjoy. They are to do good, to be rich in good works, to be generous and ready to share, thus storing up treasure for themselves as a good foundation for the future, so that they may take hold of that which is truly life

(1 Timothy 6:6-10, 17-19).

The 'present age' of which Paul speaks is the realm 'under the sun' in which the Preacher of Ecclesiastes makes his observations, draws his conclusions, lays up his treasure and settles for empty coping rather than hoping.

Fearing God lifts our eye to the Giver not the gifts. Our response will be thanks and trust. The language of contentment is thanksgiving; the tone is trust. Our attitude toward finances and possessions under the sun will be transformed. We will look at our money with different eyes. Our pay increase at work will be an opportunity to give more to his kingdom, to share with those in need. We will find greater delight in giving to kingdom causes in the name of Jesus than we will in putting a new car in our driveway. At the same time, we will appreciate the things we do have as coming to us from the hand of our God.

In one sense the stock market dive is good, serving as a vivid reminder of how quickly our hope can crumble if it rests in anything other than our God.

From early on in my marriage, my wife served as my investment counsellor. Newly married, setting up a home in our $160 a month apartment, Linda and I compared income to expenses. If it had been a boxing contest, the expenses would have had its hand raised in victory. Our income as students was no match for our bills, even with an austere standard of living.

Then my wife said something I thought absurd. She said we needed to give ten per cent of our income as a tithe to our local church. I questioned her sanity and pointed out that we didn't have enough money to pay our bills as it was. My approach would be to begin to 'tithe' when we had something left over to do it with. That led to my first tutorial in kingdom investment. Linda, who had been a Christian since eighth grade, opened the Bible to show me Jesus' principles of kingdom economics and investment strategy. I, a believer of only four months, didn't fully understand, but I knew enough to believe Jesus.

We tithed, on our net income at that point, and, sure enough, our bills were fully met every month, often in remarkable ways I would not have encountered had we employed an investment strategy based on 'under the sun' principles. God made that ninety per cent go further than the one hundred per cent ever reasonably could. Plus, the remaining ninety per cent was received with a thanksgiving and expectation infused with faith. What Linda did was bring the fear of God and obedience to his commandments as the financial regulator to our lives.

Jesus' parable about the rich fool building bigger barns counsels us to listen to the Preacher in Ecclesiastes and see the vanity of finances and possessions rooted in this world, where those material assets can be taken from us by thieves or we can be taken from our material assets by death. Instead, we are to listen to the counsel of the unnamed teacher to fear God by loving and trusting in him alone, and obeying his commands in seeking first his kingdom and righteousness, as we live for Christ and all we have is sanctified for his sake under the sun.

Questions from Qoheleth

1. When we do an inventory of our possessions, what should be our attitude toward God? How does David in 1 Chronicles 29:10-17 instruct us in this attitude?

2. What value does money have in our lives? Is money inherently evil? How do the following passages regulate money and possessions: 1 Timothy 6:1-10; Matthew 22:19-21.

3. What main lesson does Jesus teach in his parable of Luke 12:13-21? How does Ecclesiastes 5:10-16 reflect Jesus' teaching?

4. What is the relationship of money and possessions to worry in Matthew 6:19-34? Of all the contenders for idols why would Jesus highlight money (Mammon) as the contender for our hearts in Matthew 6:24? How can money be a substitute for God and for seeking first his kingdom?

5. What lessons about money and our use of it can we glean from Paul's teaching in 2 Corinthians 8:1-15? Verse 15 harkens to God's daily provision of manna. How does this relate to worry and contentment reflected in Matthew 6:34?

6. What investment principles does Paul lay out for us in 2 Corinthians 9:6-15? What does verse 11 suggest as a reason for God's entrusting us with money? How is this expressed in Ephesians 4:28?

7. Where can we find the voice of the Preacher and that of the unnamed teacher in 1 Timothy 6:17-19 and Hebrews 13:5-6? How is our attitude toward money and possessions a good litmus test for whether our perspective and portfolio are found 'under the sun' or in the age to come?

8. What is the main concern of Proverbs 30:7-9? How does this direct our prayer?

And Nehemiah, who was the governor, and Ezra the priest
and scribe, and the Levites who taught
the people said to all the people, 'This day is holy to the
LORD your God; do not mourn or weep.' For all the people
wept as they heard the words of the Law.
Then he said to them, 'Go on your way.
Eat the fat and drink sweet wine and send portions
to anyone who has nothing ready, for this day is holy
to our Lord. And do not be grieved,
for the joy of the LORD is your strength'

(Nehemiah 8:9-10).

6.
Vanity of pleasure and entertainment

Ecclesiastes is a book that speaks to every dimension of life, making our lives God-centred and God-serving in all its aspects and activities. We've exposed the main issue on the table in Ecclesiastes as idolatry, remedied by fearing the living and true God and keeping his commandments rather than being led at worst by the nihilistic worldview engendered by a fallen world and rebellious heart, or at best by a vague religious worldview that distorts God and seeks to manage or manipulate him. Not that we worship money and possessions and family in the ritualistic sense, but that we can put these things before God, making them more important than God. We can trust in them or look to them for what only God can give. In this chapter we look at another rival for allegiance and pursuit that are rightfully God's: the vanity of pleasure and entertainment. Again, listen to an excerpt from the Preacher's journal under the sun as he chronicles his observations of life in a fallen world and his efforts to deal with the futility and frustration he sees.

I said in my heart, 'Come now, I will test you with pleasure; enjoy yourself.' But behold, this also was vanity. I said of laughter, 'It is mad,' and of pleasure, 'What use is it?' I searched with my heart how to cheer my body with wine — my heart still guiding me with wisdom — and how to lay hold on folly, till I might see what was good for the children of man to do under heaven during the few days of their life...

And whatever my eyes desired I did not keep from them. I kept my heart from no pleasure, for my heart found pleasure in all my toil, and this was my reward for all my toil. Then I considered all that my hands had done and the toil I had expended in doing it, and behold, all was vanity and a striving after wind, and there was nothing to be gained under the sun

(Eccles. 2:1-3, 10-11).

What is the greatest obstacle to be overcome in the routine of everyday life? There are a good number who would suggest that the greatest obstacle is boredom. The litmus test for the value of an activity is whether it breaks the boredom barrier.

The boredom barometer touches all sorts of things. *USA Today* keeps its stories brief lest they lose our attention. Political debate consists of soundbites. We can see the value placed in entertainment. In 2005 a Supreme Court justice earned $200,000 dollars. Television's Judge Judy made $25,000,000.

The church has not been spared: the shorter the sermon the better. As soon as the twelve o'clock hour strikes, people start to squirm in their seats, their religious obligation having been fulfilled. Many people jump from church to church to be entertained like they would go from one movie to another or to the theatre with the more comfortable chairs. The mantra for attending a worship service is not 'Bless the Lord, O my soul', but 'Be blessed of the Lord, O my soul'.

Do you see the problem? Our lives as Christians become concerned with ourselves. Our relationship with Christ boils down to what he can do for me. We become driven by comfort and convenience. We're glad to serve if it doesn't demand too much of us or doesn't cause too much inconvenience. In the meantime, the church becomes weak and ineffective, and a non-factor for the redemptive kingdom of our Lord.

Serving this disposition to self is the vanity of pleasure and entertainment. It makes sense, considering the harshness of life. During times of severe distress in our country, movie ticket sales rocket. Last year was a banner year for the box office, against the backdrop of an economic crisis that saw people cashing in the change collecting in their coin jars. A two-hour escape from harsh reality provides a respite from having to contend with it. The pain of work created by the Fall is remedied by the weekend. Work becomes a necessary evil to fund what life is really all about — having fun.

Being pleasure-driven is nothing new. The Preacher practised it. The Epicureans majored in it. The Stoics eschewed it. Religious types manage it. The question is: what place does pleasure have in lives that seek and serve God? The worldview of creation, fall and redemption found in Ecclesiastes gives us our bearings.

God wired us for pleasure

God designed us for pleasure. Think of that aroma of coffee that greets you in the morning, its taste nudging you awake, its heat kick-starting your day. Even non-coffee drinkers tend to enjoy the scent of brewing coffee. Or, smell that lasagne cooking and feel your taste buds doing their warm-ups. Notice how your eyes brighten as you take in the spectrum of autumn colours or savour the sunrise at the beach.

God has designed it so that sex is not a chore but something to be enjoyed within the bonds of marriage. The idea that sex is just for making babies is wrong-headed and theologically mistaken. The religious notion that 'If it feels good, it must be wrong' doesn't understand God's design in giving us good things in life and five senses to enjoy them.

God even appeals to our desires. What did he call the land to which he was taking the Israelites? — 'a land flowing with milk and honey'. That is sensuous speech, appealing to the pleasures of the palate, rich expressions of blessing and enjoyment.

Listen to the pleasure principles observed by the Preacher in Ecclesiastes:

> Behold, what I have seen to be good and fitting is to eat and drink and find enjoyment in all the toil with which one toils under the sun the few days of his life that God has given him, for this is his lot. Everyone also to whom God has given wealth and possessions and power to enjoy them, and to accept his lot and rejoice in his toil — this is the gift of God. For he will not much remember the days of his life because God keeps him occupied with joy in his heart
>
> (Eccles. 5:18-20).

The Preacher presumes pleasure. He sees the pleasures of life as wonderful distractions to the hardship under the sun, balms to the weary soul and worn-out body. We can relate to this: think vacation, think chocolate.

God warns us of being pleasure-driven

Jackson, my daughter's longhaired dachshund, will give you no rest. If you scratch his ears and rub his fur, he won't let you stop. He puts his wet nose under your hand to compel you not to be derelict in your doggy duty. To avoid the irritant of his pestering and the discomfort of his wet nose on your skin, you resume attending to the little beast. And when it comes to eating! Jackson constantly has his nose to the ground and his tongue at the ready in search of morsels, which would explain why my dachshund's skin is loose and Jackson's is not.

We can be like that — on a constant quest for pleasure. It can even become addictive to us. We can become so sexed up we sleep with the devil in the bed of Internet pornography. We can want things so badly that in our refusal for delayed gratification we dig our grave one scoop at a time with the shovel of our credit card until we are buried in debt.

We can want to distract ourselves to such a degree that the television is never off in our home. The TV is on at dinner, so the family doesn't talk. Each child has a TV in his or her room, so that the family is not together. We don't go to the Bible study because our favourite TV show is on, DVRs notwithstanding. And entertainment ends up dominating our life and dictating our decisions.

I love to read mysteries. Reading is a good thing. There's nothing wrong with being drawn into the intricate plot of a well-written 'who-done-it'. But I found myself in one stretch reading like a chain smoker — to the neglect of other things I should be doing. Strangely enough, pleasure can become a friendly tyrant.

Pleasure and entertainment can be good, a blessing of God. But they can also be empty calories to the nutrition of a God-centred life. By abuse and misuse they can weaken us and disappoint us and can well enslave us. The Preacher observes that being driven by pleasure will only dissatisfy in the long run. He's been there; done that. He can personally attest to it.

We hear what he's saying. Here and elsewhere, the Preacher tells us how he tried to find lasting, meaningful joy in drinking and sex, in money and things, in people serving him. He did not deny himself anything that his senses fancied, as he unabashedly admits: 'And whatever my eyes desired I did not keep from them' (Eccles. 2:10). But in all these self-seeking pleasures he came up empty. The vanity part comes in when the pleasures of life become our life, or at least the most important thing for us, driving us and dominating our schedules and agendas. Entertainment can become unprincipled, unregulated and our master.

The constant pursuit of pleasures through entertainments to avoid boredom, pain or emptiness does nothing but warp life, mess up priorities and sap our energy like a sugar high and drive us to find the next fix. Its consequences show up in our lives, our homes and in the effectiveness of the church for the sake of Christ's kingdom.

God woos us to true delight

God has something better for us. The unnamed teacher directs our eyes beyond the confines of the fallen created order to the God who is and who wired us for pleasure but has spoken to direct us in his ways.

Pleasure should be received as a gift of God, but regulated by his commands. Sex is something to be enjoyed — but in the confines of marriage. God gave us taste buds to delight in the variety of foods — but gluttony is a sin. Eve saw the fruit. It was good and desirable. But its appeal and availability did not mean it was okay to partake. Healthy pleasure has boundaries and is to be accompanied by the chaperone of God's truth and Spirit.

God puts eternal truths and kingdom values in terms of our desires, drives and delights. We are to hunger after righteousness, thirst after the knowledge of God, savour the word of truth. How does the psalmist express the delight of every word that proceeds from the mouth of our God? 'More to be desired are they than gold, even much fine gold; sweeter also than honey and drippings of the honeycomb' (Psalm 19:10). God's law is something we should crave, cherishing it for its source and partaking of it by our obedience.

Christian principles of love and sacrifice are decidedly other-oriented. In a God-centred, God-serving life, pleasure is often the victim offered up on the altar of sacrifice, where we give of our time, our comfort, our desires, to serve others. Of course, in its most mature state, sacrifice itself becomes pleasurable. Our Lord Jesus exemplified this.

Therefore, since we are surrounded by so great a cloud of witnesses, let us also lay aside every weight, and sin which clings so closely, and let us run with endurance the race that is set before us, looking to Jesus, the founder and perfecter of our faith, who for the *joy* that was set before him endured the cross, despising the shame, and is seated at the right hand of the throne of God.

Consider him who endured from sinners such hostility against himself, so that you may not grow weary or fainthearted

(Hebrews 12:1-3, emphasis added).

Our ultimate delight should be God himself. 'Delight yourself in the Lord,' the Scriptures invite us. 'Taste and see that the Lord is good.' A big point of contention in churches today is whether worship should be entertaining. The answer is an unequivocal 'yes', it should be. It's intended to be. Think about it. If we delight in our God and his glory and grace, then worship that is God-centred will necessarily be entertaining. It will be thoroughly enjoyable because we thrill to sing the praises of our God. We receive the Word preached with taste buds that pop at his truth. We engage ourselves in corporate prayer that interacts with the God of creation who desires a relationship with us, and we react to such prayer in our inner being as we would to conversing with someone we deeply love. We relish the thought of unbelievers in our midst hearing the gospel of Jesus Christ. People in my congregation have said, 'My dad is going to be here today and he's not a believer,' and they are thrilled at the prospect.

We ourselves take tremendous pleasure in hearing that old, old story again that bathes our parched and weary souls with refreshing grace and corrects our attitude toward our standing before God that is always going out of alignment, away from grace and toward self-righteousness. Like going to a chiropractor for a skeletal adjustment, it feels good to get things back in line and working as they should, with life flowing from being better connected to the Head. A genuine recognition of grace will prompt cheerful giving as an act of worship. True worship is tremendously entertaining to God's saints — provided they indeed are seeking God and he is the object of their worship.

When it comes to our Christian lives, pain-avoidance or pleasure-seeking cannot drive our decisions or dictate our direction. Jesus' food was to do the will of him who sent him and that food was a delicacy to him. The Christian life is one of suffering, of cost. Look at Jesus. Look at Paul. But even with that suffering comes pleasure. We rejoice that we suffer for the name of Christ.

God gives us pleasures to enjoy, but he also gives us commands to regulate those pleasures. In this world under the sun, as with Eve at the tree of the knowledge of good and evil, the tempter lurks to seduce us by appealing to our desires in order to rob us of the highest pleasure of God himself.

An obituary appeared in the newspaper. It was about a guy named Dave Freeman. The obituary spoke of his attending the Academy Awards ceremony, running with the bulls in

Pamplona, taking a voodoo pilgrimage in Haiti, bungee jumping on the island of Vanuatu. All those are found on the list of activities in Dave Freeman's book, *100 Things to Do Before You Die*. 'This life is a short journey,' the book says, 'how can you make sure you fill it with the most fun...?' Dave Freeman didn't make it through his list. He died from a fall in his home. He was forty-seven years old.

What will your obituary say? Will it describe your heart for Christ? Will it speak of your investment in Christ's kingdom? Will the lordship of Jesus be conspicuous in your life? Will your obituary say you gave your time selflessly in love for God and neighbour? Or will it list among your accomplishments that you watched every episode of *Lost*, that you managed to spend 60% of your life sleeping or made it to level 40 of your favourite video game, and you departed without suffering — just as you tried to live your life. The draft of the apostle Paul's obituary charts a different course, driven by a different motive.

> For I am already being poured out as a drink offering, and the time of my departure has come. I have fought the good fight, I have finished the race, I have kept the faith. Henceforth there is laid up for me the crown of righteousness, which the Lord, the righteous judge, will award to me on that Day, and not only to me but also to all who have loved his appearing
> (2 Timothy 4:6-8).

God is not saying not to watch sports, or you can watch but you're not allowed to enjoy it. But he is saying that we cannot live for entertainment as a substitute for him or as an escape from the angst of a fallen world as though there were no hope. As Christians, our ultimate delight must be in the Lord our God and our ultimate goal to glorify and enjoy him in the redemptive reality of a life found in Jesus Christ.

Questions from Qoheleth

1. What value does the Preacher see in pleasure, both in itself and as a diversion? What are some of the things he mentions in which to find enjoyment? According to Ecclesiastes 2:1-2, where does pleasure fail?

2. How does pleasure function under the sun? What is the difference between being driven by pleasure and delighting in it?

3. What are some biblical illustrations of God that appeal to those things that give us pleasure? What does this say about the legitimacy of pleasure in our lives?

4. What are some ways legitimate pleasure found in life can become misused or abused? How do sins like lust or greed or covetousness contribute to this abuse?

5. How does the account of Moses in Hebrews 11:23-26 contrast fleeting pleasure with enduring pleasure? How else would you describe this contrast? How is this supremely illustrated in Jesus in Hebrews 12:1-3? How is pleasure revolutionized for us by Jesus' example?

6. How has a preoccupation with pleasure and entertainment intruded on our chief end as human beings, in the disciplines of daily life, and in our assembly for corporate worship?

7. Is corporate worship to be entertaining? Explain your reasoning. How has this entertainment been misdirected?

8. How does God use pleasure as a motivator in our lives? How does Isaiah 55:1-3 illustrate this? What else does this passage say to us about that which gives us delight?

9. How does Psalm 16 speak of pleasure from the perspective of fearing God?

10. If you were to divide your daily activities into proportions, what percentage would entertainment have? How would fear of God and obedience to his commandments reshape and sanctify that part of your life?

Vanity of pleasure and entertainment

11. What part do the proprietors of Vanity Fair have in the use of your time? How is pleasure the perfect bait for the devil's snares?

12. How does Ephesians 5:1-21 speak to this issue for you as a citizen of heaven and pilgrim through the town of Vanity? Considering Ephesians 5:3-4 and 5:8-9, how are we more tolerant of evil and unconcerned for holiness in our day in what we allow ourselves to be exposed to in music, movies, television and other forms of entertainment? What dangers does this present to us individually and to the church? How would the unnamed teacher counsel us?

There shall come forth a shoot
from the stump of Jesse,
and a branch from his roots shall bear fruit.
*And the Spirit of the L*ORD *shall rest upon him,*
the Spirit of wisdom and understanding,
the Spirit of counsel and might,
*the Spirit of knowledge and the fear of the L*ORD.
*And his delight shall be in the fear of the L*ORD.
He shall not judge by what his eyes see,
or decide disputes by what his ears hear
(Isaiah 11:1-3).

And Jesus increased in wisdom and in stature
and in favour with God and man
(Luke 2:52).

7.

Vanity of education and wisdom

The Bible contains many kinds of literature types from historical narrative to apocalyptic writing. Among those genres is 'wisdom literature'. You see it in certain psalms like Psalm 1, called a 'wisdom psalm'. Psalm 90 prays for a heart of wisdom. The book of Proverbs is part of the wisdom genre, as is Ecclesiastes. The Bible puts a high value on wisdom. Proverbs 3:13 says, 'Blessed is the one who finds wisdom.' Jesus grew in wisdom and stature and in favour with God and men. The book of James tutors us in wisdom, making it the object of our prayers, the guiding principle of our lives, the distinguishing feature among those who know God.

The Preacher in Ecclesiastes sings the praises of wisdom:

Wisdom is good with an inheritance, an advantage to those who see the sun. For the protection of wisdom is like the protection of money, and the advantage of knowledge is that wisdom preserves the life of him who has it

(7:11-12).

But, he seems to be of a mixed mind.

So I turned to consider wisdom and madness and folly. For what can the man do who comes after the king? Only what has already been done. Then I saw that there is more gain in wisdom than in folly, as there is more gain in light than in darkness. The wise person has his eyes in his head, but the fool walks in darkness. And yet I perceived that the same event happens to all of them. Then I said in my heart, 'What happens to the fool will happen to me also. Why then have I been so very wise?' And I said in my heart that this also is vanity. For of the wise as of the fool there is no enduring remembrance, seeing that in the days to come all will have been long forgotten. How the wise dies just like the fool! So I hated life, because what is done under the sun was grievous to me, for all is vanity and a striving after wind

(2:12-17).

This is one of those places where we furl our brow and scratch our head and wonder if we've found a contradiction in the Bible. How does our interpretive key serve us in sorting out this mixed message?

The Preacher is a religious observer on life. He writes what he observes in this created world that has been made dysfunctional by sin, a world 'under the sun'. He knows wisdom is supposed to be a good thing. But he looks around him and he observes that the wise man is no better off than the fool.

If we look under the sun, don't we see the same thing? We put a value on education. Yet we see the high school dropout making vast sums of money in a rock band, and someone with a Ph.D. flipping burgers. We see the wise man carefully investing his money yet losing it all in a free-falling stock market, while the guy who stuffed his savings in his mattress is still solvent. And where is God in all this? Doesn't God bless wisdom? Isn't that what Psalm 1 tells us?

Vanity of education and wisdom

Blessed is the man who walks not in the counsel of the wicked, nor stands in the way of sinners, nor sits in the seat of scoffers; but his delight is in the law of the LORD, and on his law he meditates day and night.

He is like a tree planted by streams of water that yields its fruit in its season, and its leaf does not wither. In all that he does, he prospers

(Psalm 1:1-3).

But it sure doesn't look that way. How do we make sense of this? By employing the two vantage points given us in the book of Ecclesiastes: the Preacher's, who makes observations we can all relate to under the sun, and the unnamed teacher's, who brings the perspective of faith that looks beyond the fallen created order to the God who is and who reigns.

God himself tells us about two kinds of wisdom. James introduces us to both of them:

Who is wise and understanding among you? By his good conduct let him show his works in the meekness of wisdom. But if you have bitter jealousy and selfish ambition in your hearts, do not boast and be false to the truth. This is not the wisdom that comes down from above, but is earthly, unspiritual, demonic. For where jealousy and selfish ambition exist, there will be disorder and every vile practice. But the wisdom from above is first pure, then peaceable, gentle, open to reason, full of mercy and good fruits, impartial and sincere. And a harvest of righteousness is sown in peace by those who make peace

(James 3:13-18).

Let's sort out these two kinds of wisdom from the two vantage points in the book of Ecclesiastes, looking at the fear of man and the fear of God.

Fear of man is the beginning of earthly wisdom

The Preacher in Ecclesiastes begins his observations with a search for wisdom.

> I the Preacher have been king over Israel in Jerusalem. And I applied my heart to seek and to search out by wisdom all that is done under heaven. It is an unhappy business that God has given to the children of man to be busy with. I have seen everything that is done under the sun, and behold, all is vanity and a striving after wind
>
> (Eccles. 1:12-14).

He tried to figure things out under the sun, looking to discern some sort of pattern. He wasn't a teenager who thought he knew everything. He had a great wealth of experience under his belt. He had accumulated a lot of knowledge and had the wherewithal of common sense to put it together. But it wasn't getting him any further in understanding things.

Wisdom of man, the way that seems right to a man, the appearance of wisdom to which James alludes, tries to make sense of life without respect to God. It has a different origin and a different orientation. It tries to find answers in the ingenuity of man.

In the 1960s television comedy *Gilligan's Island* (the *Lost* of my generation) the crew and passengers of the *Minnow* were shipwrecked on a remote island. If anybody was going to get them off that island, who was it going to be? The millionaire married couple, the Howes, with their money? The movie star, Ginger, with her beauty? The big, strong Skipper with his experience and leadership? Certainly not Gilligan, unless he inadvertently bumbled his way off the island. Who was the most likely candidate? The Professor, of course. Science was the hope.

We continue to look to science and the innovations of man to find answers for life and hope for the problems we face under the sun. When your perspective on life does not go beyond the sun, does not extend beyond the created order, you turn to something else. As with the Preacher, we search for meaning. We are driven to make sense of things, with God or without him.

A poster boy of man-centred wisdom is Charles Darwin. Darwin rejected the notion of a Creator God so he developed an evolutionary hypothesis as a substitute in his quest to make sense of things. A hypothesis is a scientific theory that stands or falls on empirical evidence, but evolutionary theory seems to operate to the beat of a different drum.

In her excellent book, *Total Truth*, Nancy Pearcey describes the baseless and contrived efforts of evolutionary proponents to manufacture evidence for its substitute for the Creator God. She cites examples of known frauds, such as Haeckel's manipulated sketches of embryos and the staging of peppered moths in England to showcase natural selection, in order to point out not only the desperate efforts of scientists to support the theory of evolution and persuade those who read the textbooks, but also the flawed approach to real science that follows the evidence to support or not support a hypothesis. So what we find is this, as Pearcey puts it: 'Darwinian evolution is not so much an empirical finding as a deduction from a naturalistic worldview.'

In his movie, *Expelled*, Ben Stein shows how secular scientists, trying their best to make sense and find order under the sun without reference to the Creator, not only give no credence to the prospect of intelligent design but won't even allow it at the table for discussion. Why? Because it is presuppositionally ruled out of hand, violating the rules laid down by those who confine themselves to a naturalistic view of life explored by scientific method. For such there is no fear of God in their eyes.

Real science, on the other hand, explores and discovers and chronicles God's creation. The Preacher, who collected and chronicles his observations under the sun, at least was honest in his descriptions. He neither tried to explain away God nor to force facts to serve his own agenda.

Knowledge and education do have value. They engage us in our world. They enhance our appreciation of life. They reflect the struggle we have to make sense of things and pursue the quest for meaning. But worldly wisdom and knowledge apart from the one in whom all knowledge resides and holds together are impotent to achieve their ends. Foolishness masquerading as wisdom cannot give life meaning or be our salvation. The unnamed teacher tells us:

> The words of the wise are like goads, and like nails firmly fixed are the collected sayings; they are given by one Shepherd. My son, beware of anything beyond these. Of making many books there is no end, and much study is a weariness of the flesh
>
> (12:11-12).

The facts of life are neither autonomous nor disembodied. Rather, there is one who speaks not merely to fill the head for information, but as a Shepherd to direct, protect and provide for the life lived under the sun in our spiritual formation.

Fear of God is the beginning of spiritual wisdom

I admit that I am mechanically challenged. When I undertake a project of fixing something or putting something together, it's not unusual for me to have to take it apart again and try to get it right the next time. Recently, the bulb that illuminates the dashboard clock in my car burned out. It's one of those little button bulbs. You would think it would not be a problem. How difficult could that be to replace? It took me hours. The bulb worked for a couple of weeks and then the clock went dark again. I discovered the bulb in a compartment where it had fallen. My problem was that I had the part but no directions for how to install it. Instead of trying to work it out for myself, I would have got it right by knowing the manufacturer's design and following their directions.

That's the way it works in knowing and understanding creation. We need to recognize its Creator and follow his direction. Wisdom works within the confines of the revelation of God, with the fear of God as its starting point.

Fear of God investigates and interprets a God-centred creation. Fear of God is not afraid to see and admit intelligent design. Fear of God knows that designer as the God who reveals himself in his tapestry of creation and in the record of his Word.

Fear of God recognizes and gives glory to God as Creator, and fear of God recognizes and gives glory to God as Redeemer. Our Creator is our Redeemer. If we believe in a naturalistic view of creation then we will trust in a naturalistic view of redemption in which we somehow save ourselves, if there is anything to be saved from. Death and decay become natural rather than unnatural, answered by naturalistic means rather than supernatural.

This is what our God says to that. Listen to Paul's contrast of wisdom from below, under the sun, and wisdom from above:

And I, when I came to you, brothers, did not come proclaiming to you the testimony of God with lofty speech or wisdom. For I decided to know nothing among you except Jesus Christ and him crucified. And I was with you in weakness and in fear and much trembling, and my speech and my message were not in plausible words of wisdom, but in demonstration of the Spirit and of power, that your faith might not rest in the wisdom of men but in the power of God

(1 Corinthians 2:1-5).

Feel the gravitational pull of grace as Paul distinguishes between 'plausible words of wisdom' and the wisdom bound up in the ways and means of God, most conspicuously exhibited in the cross of Christ.

How did Gilligan and the others get off the island by the series finale? They never did. It wasn't until years later when the cast had a television reunion that they were rescued from the island. But do you know what saved them? It wasn't money, beauty, brawn or chance. It was the creator, the writer, who rescued them. So Jesus Christ, the image of the invisible God, by whom and through whom all things were created, became our Redeemer by the sacrifice of the cross. Paul explains the fertility of the wisdom with respect to God as opposed to the futility of wisdom that begins and ends with man.

For consider your calling, brothers: not many of you were wise according to worldly standards, not many were powerful, not many were of noble birth. But God chose what is foolish in the world to shame the wise; God chose what is weak in the world to shame the strong; God chose what is low and despised in the world, even things that are not, to bring to nothing things that are, so that no human being might boast in the presence of God. He is the source of your life in Christ Jesus, whom God made our wisdom and our righteousness and sanctification and redemption. Therefore, as it is written, 'Let the one who boasts, boast in the Lord'

(1 Corinthians 1:26-31).

Vanity of education and wisdom

Any other wisdom for salvation is but vanity and chasing after wind.

How would you define 'wisdom'? Various Christian writers have their definitions:

- experiential knowledge;
- skill for life;
- the effort to discover order in human life.

What is the problem with each of these definitions? Where is the reference to God? The definitions are right to a degree but they are incomplete. The wisdom God commends is wisdom that begins with God and flows from God and moves toward God. Such wisdom operates in the fear of God, recognizing him, honouring him, serving him, seeking him, submitting to him.

We could put it this way: the wisdom we are to seek is not 'street smarts' to navigate the roadways of life. Wisdom is the compass of God where due north is the glory of God and the magnetic pull is the fear of God due his name. The writer of Proverbs gives us our orientation.

> 'The fear of the LORD is the beginning of knowledge'
> (Prov. 1:7);

> 'The fear of the LORD is the beginning of wisdom'
> (Prov. 9:10).

What these verses say is that the way we size things up in life, and the choices we make, have reference to God and so have a moral and spiritual dimension to them, whether it's for whom we vote at election time, or what we choose to watch on TV, or how we deal with a job loss, or how we handle conflict in the home. Wisdom is not just knowledge or knowledge with experience. Wisdom from above that finds its point of reference beyond the confines of 'under the sun' sees *God's* world and seeks *God's* ways — the zenith of which is Jesus Christ, in whom are found the treasures of the wisdom and knowledge of God.

Questions from Qoheleth

1. We live in an information age. In what way is information seen as an avenue to life, to power, even to salvation? If knowledge is viewed as a saviour, then what would be the problem to be saved from?

2. What is the difference between wisdom and knowledge? How are they related? How does the fear of God influence both? How does 1 Corinthians 3:18-20 speak of this?

3. What two types of wisdom does James contrast in James 3:13-18? What does James put in a profile of each? What is the outcome of each?

4. How can service projects be worthwhile and how can they be worthless for the religion God desires? How can our acts of service operate in the fear of God? What would characterize service that seeks God and service that seeks self? How do Jesus' interactions with the Pharisees make the distinction?

5. How does Psalm 139, a psalm that cultivates fear of God through the subject of knowledge, contrast our knowledge with God's? How does the psalmist react to the limitations of his knowledge? How does he respond to God's knowledge (Ps. 139:17-18, 23-24)? In what way does Romans 11:33-36 make the same contrast and provoke the same response?

6. What does Paul describe as the source and goal and nature of knowledge in 1 Corinthians 1:18-31 and 2:1-16?

7. For what knowledge does Paul pray in Ephesians 1:16-23; Ephesians 3:14-19; Philippians 1:9-11; Colossians 1:9-14; and Peter describe

in 2 Peter 1:2-9? How would a wisdom from above and knowledge rooted in the mind of God affect your life and living under the sun?

8. In keeping with Bunyan's account of the proprietors of Vanity Fair and knowledge as one of its offerings, what is the challenge for us in our pilgrimage under the sun according to 2 Corinthians 10:3-5? How does Colossians 2:6-8 speak of this?

And the Pharisees and the scribes asked him,
'Why do your disciples not walk according to the tradition
of the elders,
but eat with defiled hands?'
And he said to them, 'Well did Isaiah prophesy
of you hypocrites, as it is written,
"This people honours me with their lips,
but their heart is far from me;
in vain do they worship me,
teaching as doctrines the commandments of men"'
(Mark 7:5-7).

8.

Vanity of religion and service

In 2008 the Philadelphia region in the US saw two raucous celebrations. The first was the Philadelphia Phillies winning the baseball World Series. People were dancing in the streets. Tee shirts and fan gear flew off the shelves. The second was the election of Barack Obama as the forty-fourth President of the United States. People were dancing in the streets. Tee shirts and political memorabilia were being scooped up as part of the historic moment.

But not all were celebrating — fans of the Phillies' opponents, the Tampa Bay Devil Rays, for example. Many deeply invested in politics felt their hopes dashed, afraid that the moral fabric of our country, already threadbare, would become completely unravelled.

That begs the question: where is our hope? What exactly is our hope? What had changed with the political shift in the land? Had Christ changed? Had his promises changed? Had the church's mission changed?

T. M. Moore shakes us with the cold water of redemptive reality to our face.

For three decades conservative Christians have believed that the way to moral retrenchment and cultural change was through the government. We've managed to get the right people in office and on the courts, and still the erosion of traditional values and the decline of our culture continues. We just don't get it. Change comes through revival, which comes at God's pleasure, pursuant to His people's repenting of their sins and pleading with Him for renewal.

(*Crosfigell*)

Moore raises an issue, a matter of concern observed by the Preacher in the book of Ecclesiastes as he takes note of life 'under the sun'. What place does religion, with its spirituality and service, have in this fallen world? Or, to put it in terms of the major concern of the book of Ecclesiastes: What does religion look like without the fear of God at its heart?

Ecclesiastes leads us to three characterizations of religion that radically affect our hope and practice as Christ's church.

Fundamental religion

Connecting the words 'fundamental' and 'religion' can lead our minds in any number of directions. We can think of religion that adheres to the fundamentals of the Christian faith: the Bible as the literal Word of God, the deity of Christ, the virgin birth, the reality of miracles and the supernatural, the death of Jesus as a substitute to atone for the sins of his sheep, and the bodily resurrection of Jesus Christ from the dead. Or, we can think of fundamentalism where the atmosphere of religion is deprived of life-giving grace, and religion is summed up in terms of the externals of what a person does and doesn't do. Or, our minds could turn to fundamental extremists who carry out terrorist attacks in the name of religion.

But the meaning of 'fundamental' here refers to religion being fundamental to our existence as beings created in the image of God. God created us as religious beings, worshippers. The apostle Paul, in speaking to the cultural elite of his day, the religious think tank, observes, as does the Preacher in Ecclesiastes, that people are religious.

> So Paul, standing in the midst of the Areopagus, said: 'Men of Athens, I perceive that in every way you are very religious. For as I passed along and observed the objects of your worship, I found also an altar with this inscription, "To the unknown god." What therefore you worship as unknown, this I proclaim to you'
>
> (Acts 17:22-23).

Augustine said that our hearts are restless until they find rest in the living and true God, but as religious beings we seek to satisfy our restless hearts and find peace in that which is not God and which can never satisfy. Throughout the book of Ecclesiastes runs an undercurrent of man in relationship to God. The core question, though, is: what will we worship and what do we hope to achieve by our religious practice?

My wife and I spent the evening recently with some members of my church who were home from a two-year stint in India, where the husband was on assignment for work. They told of the hundreds of gods which are part of the religious fabric of the society and related the stories of how some of these gods came into being, including one of how a human body came to have the head of an elephant. The backgrounds of the various gods could vary with the oral tradition indigenous to a particular region. But whatever the source, gods and an atmosphere of religion pervaded the culture.

We might think of ourselves as twenty-first-century Western sophisticates beyond such nonsense. But if you were to conduct a quiz on a person's view of God you would often find that there is some conception of God, resulting in some impact or benefit to that person's life. People create a power higher than themselves, often manufactured in their own image and controlled by their own design.

All who bear the image of God are worshippers in some sense. We are religious people driven to serve some cause for the value we think important. Our religion takes some form.

Futile religion

The Preacher sees the folly of just going through the motions.

> Guard your steps when you go to the house of God. To draw near to listen is better than to offer the sacrifice of fools, for they do not know that they are doing evil
> (Eccles. 5:1).

Jesus did the same thing in speaking to the religious fundamentalists of his day, the Pharisees. He quoted from the Old Testament to show that the problem of empty religion existed then and continues to exist.

> 'This people honours me with their lips,
>   but their heart is far from me;
> in vain do they worship me,
>   teaching as doctrines the commandments of men'
> (Matt. 15:8-9).

What happened was that people made religion something it was not. Instead of a religion where God was at the centre and man served God, religion became a way for God to serve man, and man to control God. We see it with the ancient Israelites who took the Ark of the Covenant into battle against the Philistines.

> The Philistines drew up in line against Israel, and when the battle spread, Israel was defeated by the Philistines, who killed about four thousand men on the field of battle. And when the troops came to the camp, the elders of Israel said, 'Why has the LORD defeated us today before the Philistines? Let us bring the ark of the covenant of the LORD here from Shiloh, that it may come among us and save us from the power of our enemies'
>
> (1 Samuel 4:2-3).

Here we see religious practice divorced from God, more superstitious than supernatural, more in keeping with the occult than the Creator who is to be worshipped and served.

What does futile religion look like? It is trying to find life, substance and meaning through a religious system rather than a relationship with God through Jesus Christ. This form of Christianity is no different from Buddhism, Islam or Judaism. If we are honest with ourselves, our religious practice can degenerate into mindless prayers and meaningless routines, and our religious activity operates more according to the principle of karma than Christ — what goes around comes around. Be a nice boy or girl and God will reward you accordingly. The Preacher observes the disconnection between religious effort, even though sincere, and its outcome.

> Though a sinner does evil a hundred times and prolongs his life, yet I know that it will be well with those who fear God, because they fear before him. But it will not be well with the wicked, neither will he prolong his days like a shadow, because he does not fear before God.

Making sanity out of vanity

There is a vanity that takes place on earth, that there are righteous people to whom it happens according to the deeds of the wicked, and there are wicked people to whom it happens according to the deeds of the righteous. I said that this also is vanity

(Eccles. 8:12-14).

The Preacher cannot even find sanity in religious prescription. It's unpredictable.

People involve themselves in religion and service because it's good for the family. How often do we see couples return to church when a baby comes along? Sometimes the non-churchgoer will make sure their baby is baptized but that pretty much exhausts their religious participation. After all, we don't want to take this religious stuff too far.

What motivates religious observance? Going to church may scratch a spiritual itch or satisfy a routine inculcated by family practice growing up. How many times have we seen people remain at a church that has long since abandoned the gospel and any biblical moorings, just because their parents and their parents' parents went there?

People may feel like they are contributing by involvement in various ministries, perhaps even as a way to assuage a sense of guilt, perhaps as a means of being a contributing member of society. The words of encouragement they hear from the pulpit may be the 'pep' talk they need to keep on going another week in the disheartening and demoralizing heat under the sun, some way to dispel the vanity of life. Perhaps, religion serves as a vehicle for the health and wealth they cannot find by chasing after wind. For them, God is a cosmic vending machine. They reach for God under the sun but without the fear of God.

Religion cannot exist for the sake of religion. The church in America and elsewhere nowadays is in deep distress, busy with religion, but almost unrecognizable to the God who inhabits the praises of his people; more big business than Christ's business, a non-factor because it trades in the commodities of the world rather than Christ's kingdom; it is just another offering of Vanity Fair.

Jesus constantly sparred with the religious leaders of his day, who promoted godless, man-made religion. He quotes from Isaiah the prophet and in so doing shows that there is nothing new under the sun.

Now when the Pharisees gathered to him, with some of the scribes who had come from Jerusalem, they saw that some of his disciples ate with hands that were defiled, that is, unwashed. (For the Pharisees and all the Jews do not eat unless they wash their hands, holding to the tradition of the elders, and when they come from the market-place, they do not eat unless they wash. And there are many other traditions that they observe, such as the washing of cups and pots and copper vessels and dining couches.) And the Pharisees and the scribes asked him, 'Why do your disciples not walk according to the tradition of the elders, but eat with defiled hands?' And he said to them, 'Well did Isaiah prophesy of you hypocrites, as it is written,

"This people honours me with their lips,
    but their heart is far from me;
in vain do they worship me,
    teaching as doctrines the commandments of men."

'You leave the commandment of God and hold to the tradition of men.'

And he said to them, 'You have a fine way of rejecting the commandment of God in order to establish your tradition!'

(Mark 7:1-9).

Fearing God and obeying his commandments had been excised from religious practice in favour of religion contoured to the designs and desires of men, leaving nothing but futility.

Fertile religion

Contrary to this religion that has an appearance of wisdom but is devoid of power, the unnamed teacher calls us to fear God and keep his commandments, infusing a spiritual frame of reference to religious practice and to all of life. In other words, we need to look to the God whom we serve and who is able to do beyond what we could think, either through the hearts of kings and those voted into office, or apart from them.

In the book of Ephesians, the apostle Paul speaks of great power, transforming power, subduing power, power to effect change, a power resident in the church. That power is not the church wielding the Spirit, but the Spirit wielding the church in the resurrection power of Jesus Christ. In that mode, with that end, we find sure and certain hope. There resides the distinction between riding a mighty movement of God's Spirit and resorting to a monument of spirituality in an attempt to quell our fears or impregnate life with at least some measure of meaning.

True religion does not make us the chief end. True religion does not reduce religious practice or rituals to ends in themselves. True religion makes God and his glory the chief end. True religion works to exalt the name of God in worship and service.

In the late 1990s, British songwriter Matt Redman described how flat and hollow and powerless and mundane things were in his local church. In an interview he says, 'There was a dynamic missing, so the pastor did a pretty brave thing. He decided to get rid of the sound system and band for a season, and we gathered together with just our voices. His point was that we'd lost our way in worship, and the way to get back to the heart would be to strip everything away.'

Reminding his church family to be producers in worship, not just consumers, the pastor asked, 'When you come through the doors on a Sunday, what are you bringing as your offering to God?' Matt said the question initially led to some embarrassing silence, but eventually people broke into a cappella songs and heartfelt prayers, encountering God in a fresh way. 'Before long, we reintroduced the musicians and sound system, as we'd gained a new perspective that worship is all about Jesus, and he commands a response in the depths of our souls no matter what the circumstance and setting. "The Heart of Worship" simply describes what occurred.' Here is that description:

When the music fades,
all is stripped away
and I simply come;
longing just to bring
something that's of worth,
that will bless your heart.

I'll bring You more than a song,
for a song in itself
is not what You have required.
You search much deeper within
through the ways things appear,
You're looking into my heart.

I'm coming back to the heart of worship,
and it's all about You,
all about You, Jesus.
I'm sorry, Lord, for the thing I've made it,
when it's all about You,
it's all about You, Jesus.

King of endless worth,
no one could express
how much You deserve.
Though I'm weak and poor,
all I have is Yours,
every single breath.

I'll bring You more than just a song,
for a song in itself
is not what You have required.
You search much deeper within
through the way things appear,
You're looking into my heart.

I'm coming back to the heart of worship,
and it's all about You,
 all about You, Jesus.
I'm sorry, Lord, for the thing I've made it,
when it's all about You,
 it's all about You, Jesus.

Its all about you, Jesus.

Matt Redmond, 'The Heart of Worship
(When the music fades)',
©1999 Thankyou Music (PRS). All rights reserved.
Used by permission.

Matt Redman's conviction and quest had to do with restoring the fear of God to the church and Christ to Christianity, with the church being the church in the world, positioned in the midst of Vanity Fair but not part of it, the church where Christ himself lives by his Spirit.

Government is important, but government is impotent for the change and the impact Christ seeks. We need to take seriously our role as Christian citizens. But our hope is not in government. Our hope is in God. Christ's church needs to be the church, whether it's in the USA, in China or in India. We cannot go back to pre-Reformation medieval times when the church sought control of the State. The church must be the church. The power of the church is not exercised in the voting booth but in the prayer closet. In a recent prayer letter, ministry leader Archie Parrish asserts: 'I believe the best and maybe the last hope for America is God-sent revival and revitalized local churches. Revival means to restore something to the purpose for which it's made.' The influence of the church is not exerted at election season but in season and out of season, bearing witness to Christ, being salt and light in the world.

As Christians in society God calls us to pay and to pray. In my family devotions on a recent Election Day, I led in a study of Romans 13.

> Let every person be subject to the governing authorities. For there is no authority except from God, and those that exist have been instituted by God ... Pay to all what is owed to them: taxes to whom taxes are owed, revenue to whom revenue is owed, respect to whom respect is owed, honour to whom honour is owed
>
> (Romans 13:1, 7).

Paul issues a similar call in his first letter to Timothy.

> First of all, then, I urge that supplications, prayers, intercessions, and thanksgivings be made for all people, for kings and all who are in high positions, that we may lead a peaceful and quiet life, godly and dignified in every way
>
> (1 Timothy 2:1-2).

Our God reigns. He directs the hearts of kings. He raises up rulers and kingdoms and he brings them down — all for his purposes. He is the King of kings. God raised up Cyrus to allow the Jews to return to the promised land after the exile. God raised up Caesar and the Roman government to crucify the Christ. God sent Daniel and the exiles to Babylon to be an influence for righteousness and, years later, wise men from the east would come to search for the Christ child, who would be the Saviour of the world, good news of great joy to all men, Jew and Gentile alike. God designs to use the church as his agent for change. But we must *be* the church, practising a religion that knows the living and true God and seeks his glory, by his strength, for his ends in this world, not in worldly religious economics that would try to control God but in the heavenly economics of grace that seek and serve him despite appearances.

The local YMCA to which I have belonged for years was moving to an expanded facility. To encourage members to move along with it, they offered a free tee shirt. On the shirt was a logo that held three icons, one each for spirit, mind and body. The image for body was a dumbbell. The outline of a person in a lotus position represented the mind. But it was the graphic for 'spirit' that particularly caught my eye. It held the familiar religious symbol of the chi and rho, over which was superimposed an open book with the biblical reference John 17:21 inscribed on it.

That reference is from Jesus' high priestly prayer given in his upper room discourse.

'...that they may all be one, just as you, Father, are in me, and I in you, that they also may be in us, so that the world may believe that you have sent me'

(John 17:21).

134

That was the YMCA's mission that belongs to a day in the past, when it was conspicuously the Young Men's Christian Association. Is that true of the church? Is our Christianity in name only? Does our religion belong more to a 'churchianity' that functions under the sun with little or distorted reference to God. Have we forgotten, or suppressed, what the one whose name we bear desires of us?

I contacted the director of the new YMCA in my area to point out that in their programming they offered classes and activities for the mind and the body but nothing for the spirit. I encouraged them as part of their mission statement to provide offerings that would address the spiritual dimension. I told them I'd be glad to teach a course on the basics of Christianity and am pursuing the prospect.

That's just what Matt Redmond does in his song, 'The Heart of Worship'. He looks to restore religion to the purpose given it by God.

When the music fades,
all is stripped away
and I simply come;
longing just to bring
something that's of worth,
that will bless Your heart...

> *I'm coming back to the heart of worship,
> and it's all about You, Jesus.*

Questions from Qoheleth

1. How would you describe your spiritual disciplines of reading the Bible and prayer? What does this say about your spiritual health? What prognosis does it hold for your future?

2. What does Jesus lay out as his fitness goal and regimen for you as his disciple in Ephesians 4:1-24? What is necessary in your mentality and practice to move you toward that goal?

3. In what sense are we religious beings? How does this manifest itself in the world's cultures? How does Christianity differ from 'under the sun' religions?

4. How does the Preacher in Ecclesiastes exhibit a works righteousness mentality? How would the correction of the teacher in Ecclesiastes 12:13-14 discredit the Preacher's mentality and promote grace-based righteousness? What bigger horizon is necessary to arrive at this conclusion (cf. Rom. 3:9-31)?

5. How does the account of Paul in Athens (Acts 17:22-34) show us the tendency to make God in their own image? What is Paul's corrective? On what basis does Paul make that corrective under the sun?

6. How can religious practice be vanity, a chasing after wind? How can it be of value? What does Jesus say in Mark 7:1-13 to highlight the vanity and the value? How can we try to find fulfilment and salvation in doing good works and religious ritual apart from Christ?

7. How is the religious practice of the Israelites in 1 Samuel 4:1-11 an example of superstitious religion? How can we do the very same thing? How can this practice foster presumption and false hope (cf. Matt. 7:21-23)?

8. Why would you say the church is ineffective for the sake of the kingdom? How would you assess your own faithfulness and effectiveness? What needs to change? How can Psalm 80 and Psalm 85 serve as guides for our prayer toward this change?

Have you not known? Have you not heard?
The LORD is the everlasting God,
the Creator of the ends of the earth.
He does not faint or grow weary;
his understanding is unsearchable.
He gives power to the faint,
and to him who has no might he increases strength.
Even youths shall faint and be weary,
and young men shall fall exhausted;
but they who wait for the LORD
shall renew their strength;
they shall mount up with wings like eagles;
they shall run and not be weary;
they shall walk and not faint
(Isaiah 40:28-31).

9.
Vanity of strength and beauty

My daughter worked at a fitness centre, where she encountered Jim. Jim comes in every day. He has to more shuffle than walk, as his muscle mass impedes an ordinary gait. Jim is a serious weightlifter. His dedication would not allow much to sidetrack him from his workouts. He tore his abdominal muscles but he wouldn't miss a workout. Pretty soon he developed a bulge in his abdominal area. It was his intestines protruding through a torn abdominal wall. Jim would just push the bulge back in place and keep plugging away. After a bodybuilding competition he thought he'd better have it checked out. Jim had waited too long, though. A large part of his intestines had become gangrenous and had to be removed. Jim lived to lift.

Jim reminds me of a mouse I once saw that had its head caught in a mousetrap. Even as it lay dying, it continued to stick out its tongue to try and eat the peanut butter.

Both of those examples seem pretty extreme. Most of us are not that obsessed. However, we do live in a society where beauty is a god and fitness is a religion. Their 'Bibles' fill the shelves, as magazines depicting lean, muscled men and slender, toned women adorn the covers. The articles promise

to do the same for you. The greatest enemy in this religion? —
aging. Aging leads to wrinkles and weakness. Older people are
admired when they can look young, through rigorous workout
regimens or the knife of a plastic surgeon. Everything possible
is done to slow or reverse the aging process.

The Preacher in Ecclesiastes acknowledges the benefits
of youth. But he echoes what everyone who has sought to
cling onto youth discovers. No matter how healthy you eat,
no matter how much you run each day, no matter how much
you work out, no matter how much time you invest in your
appearance under the sun, your body will age and you will die.

In this chapter we trace two pursuits from the perspective
of the book of Ecclesiastes: one a chasing after wind, the other
full of promise. We can capture these pursuits in terms of two
fountains: one of youth, the other of life.

Pursuing the fountain of youth

In the chronicling of his observations under the sun the
Preacher takes note of three things related to the inexorable
march to the grave: youth, aging and death itself.

The Preacher's recognizes the value of youth, when
someone is young, supple, energetic and whose life is full of
promise.

> Rejoice, O young man, in your youth, and let your heart
> cheer you in the days of your youth. Walk in the ways
> of your heart and the sight of your eyes. But know that
> for all these things God will bring you into judgement.
>
> Remove vexation from your heart, and put away
> pain from your body, for youth and the dawn of life are
> vanity
>
> (Eccles. 11:9-10).

Vanity of strength and beauty

Youth is a good thing, the epitome of strength and vitality. Often, young people cannot imagine death. They think they are invincible. But the Preacher says they should enjoy it while they have it, because it will fade. The days before us that seem so full of promise are in reality pointless, vanity of vanities. Even legitimate youth disappoints, let alone the manufactured youth of cosmetics and cosmetic surgery that are nothing more than a coat of paint on the old car.

There's nothing wrong with keeping yourself in shape. There's nothing wrong with beauty. When my son was in high school, he and I visited Senegal. What struck us both was the dusty and drab overall feel of the place. The coast held its own miniature of the picture painted by the two vantage points of Ecclesiastes. Senegal is Africa's westernmost point. Just off shore sits Goree Island. As you can imagine, the scenery and view are breathtaking. Yet a closer look reveals cells where those slaves herded from Africa's interior were held to await ships to collect them for distribution. Real beauty defiled by fallen reality.

One of things that impressed me amidst the monochromatic feel of Dakar, the capital of Senegal, was the beauty of the women. Many were tall, dark and statuesque. But it was the way they dressed that struck me. Against their drab surroundings these women wore bright, flowing dresses, and walked erect and graceful in their display. The Preacher would see this as good to take the edge off the dismal, depressing life under the sun in a world filled with death and decay. It won't solve anything, but it will be a bright spot like flowers at a funeral, like putting lilies in the cells of those slaves waiting to be distributed for sale.

However, the Preacher notes, youth is nothing but a point on the continuum of aging. The eighteen-year-old who seemed old to the ten-year-old, himself regards thirty as 'ancient', until he reaches that age. How many of us have changed our threshold for what is 'old'? Life under the sun is the descent into the shadow of futility, tempered by euphemisms like 'golden years', measuring age by however many 'years young'. Youth and aging are on the same continuum of chasing after wind. The Preacher's observation? 'So if a person lives many years, let him rejoice in them all; but let him remember that the days of darkness will be many. All that comes is vanity' (11:8).

Rejoice in your days, making the most of them. Take your children to the park. Go on family vacations. Fill your scrapbook with memories. Check off your goals of visiting every state, or other countries. But be assured that you will experience pain and loss and emptiness, as the river of life flushes into the basin of death. *Dr 90210*, the reality television show celebrating the wonders of plastic surgery, might help with the wrinkles and the sagging, but you cannot stop yourself from wearing out or derail your steady trek to the grave.

Notice how vividly the Preacher describes aging:

Remember also your Creator in the days of your youth, before the evil days come and the years draw near of which you will say, 'I have no pleasure in them'; before the sun and the light and the moon and the stars are darkened and the clouds return after the rain, in the day when the keepers of the house tremble, and the strong men are bent, and the grinders cease because they are few, and those who look through the windows are dimmed, and the doors on the street are shut — when the sound of the grinding is low, and one rises up at the sound of a bird, and all the daughters of song are brought low — they are afraid also of what is high, and terrors are in the way; the almond tree blossoms, the grasshopper drags itself along, and desire fails, because man is going to his eternal home, and the mourners go about the streets — before the silver cord is snapped, or

the golden bowl is broken, or the pitcher is shattered at
the fountain, or the wheel broken at the cistern, and the
dust returns to the earth as it was, and the spirit returns
to God who gave it

(12:1-7).

The Preacher gives picture after picture of the movement
from youth to old age, like a couple celebrating fifty years of
marriage might pull out their wedding album to see what was.
The house that was so new and beautiful starts falling apart,
while life goes on around it. You go to someone's funeral; all
the while the traffic rushes by and the world does not seem to
notice. It will be no different at your funeral. The world will
not stop. The silver chain and the golden bowl so resplendent
in beauty and permanence snap and break, just like the clothes
you bought new but which are now worn and tattered and
ready for the local Goodwill store, or charity shop. The
strong man stoops with age and the eye grows dim. The
tennis champion who held high the trophy of his conquest,
now can barely shuffle to the centre court. The woman who
wrote books, was in demand on the speaking circuit, the
embodiment of competency, is now in the grip of Alzheimer's
and no longer recognizes her own husband.

Then there is the terminus itself under the sun, the end of
the line for everyone — death, the only thing that can really
stop the aging process. As though proving his point in the
conclusions he draws from his observations under the sun, the
Preacher lays on the table the clincher.

But all this I laid to heart, examining it all, how the
righteous and the wise and their deeds are in the hand
of God. Whether it is love or hate, man does not know;
both are before him. It is the same for all, since the same
event happens to the righteous and the wicked, to the

good and the evil, to the clean and the unclean, to him who sacrifices and him who does not sacrifice. As is the good, so is the sinner, and he who swears is as he who shuns an oath. This is an evil in all that is done under the sun, that the same event happens to all. Also, the hearts of the children of man are full of evil, and madness is in their hearts while they live, and after that they go to the dead. But he who is joined with all the living has hope, for a living dog is better than a dead lion. For the living know that they will die, but the dead know nothing, and they have no more reward, for the memory of them is forgotten. Their love and their hate and their envy have already perished, and for ever they have no more share in all that is done under the sun

(9:1-6).

Taxes might be avoided but death stands alone as the certain fate under the sun, faced by pagan and believer alike, God-hater and God-fearer, human and animal. Death does not discriminate; it is an equal opportunity destroyer.

As God fashioned man, male and female, from the dust of the ground, so he formed the beasts of the field and the birds of heaven, and with them, man returns to the dust. We minimize the finality of death with stories of OBEs (out-of-body experiences), describing a welcoming light or being resuscitated to return to the land of the living. But that's not death. Death is final. Death is inevitable; like the gaping mouth of the grave, we all move toward its precipice. People say that fingernails grow after death, but that's just an illusion as the flesh around them shrivels up.

One of the sailors who accompanied Christopher Columbus on his second voyage to the New World was a man named Juan Ponce de Leon. He had heard many stories of a magical water source. People called it the 'Fountain of Youth' and said that drinking its water kept a person young. Ponce set out in search of this water source. For the next few years, he tried to find out where this 'Fountain of Youth' was. He believed he finally discovered its location. In 1513, his government-funded voyage took him to Florida. He founded a colony, but he never found the fountain of youth. That search continues to this day under the sun, whether through the surgeon's knife, the recaptured virility of a little blue pill, the latest miracle cream, or the rigors of just staying in shape to make the most out of the days we have, eager to hear the comment, 'You don't look a day over... [*your age minus ten years*].'

Pursuing the fountain of life

Yet another fountain stands before us; one that defies the shadow of death cast under the sun; one seen through the lens of the fear of God and witnessed to by hearing his commandment.

> And this is his commandment, that we believe in the name of his Son Jesus Christ and love one another, just as he has commanded us. Whoever keeps his commandments abides in him, and he in them. And by this we know that he abides in us, by the Spirit whom he has given us
>
> (1 John 3:23-24).

As we lift our eyes beyond the contorted confines of this fallen world to the God who is and who has spoken, he tells us not of a fountain of youth, but of a fountain of life. And that fountain of life is bound up in Jesus Christ (cf. John 4:13-15; 6:25-27; 7:37-38), who conquered sin, death and the grave and who promises escape from death to all who believe in his name (John 11:25-26).

In the same realism employed by the writer of Ecclesiastes, the psalmist sobers us with these words:

> Truly no man can ransom another, or give to God the price of his life, for the ransom of their life is costly and can never suffice, that he should live on for ever and never see the pit
>
> (Ps. 49:7-9).

The psalmist concludes that for those who renounce the reality of God and reject the revelation of his Word, 'Death shall be their shepherd' (Ps. 49:14).

Yet for those who by God's grace have been loved and purchased and sought, the Lord shall be their shepherd. They shall not want. God himself is with them in goodness and mercy as they walk through the valley of the shadow of death cast under the oppressive sun of this fallen world. Nothing can wrest them from the Shepherd's hand. Nothing can separate them from the love of God in Christ Jesus.

Jesus is the living water, the fountain of life, from which waters of eternal life flow. In stark contrast to the depressing and defeatist picture given by the Preacher in Ecclesiastes under the sun, the unnamed teacher directs us to the face of God and to hear his voice, a voice that speaks words of life. This God admits to disease, decay and death but says he has provided for victory over these things.

Redemptive reality leads us to find hope and life not in the bravado of youth or attempts to cling to youth but in God. Our efforts to find life and meaning and endurance in youth are misplaced, seeking hope under the sun that will only disappoint. Isaiah tutors us in the fear of God and directs us to the hope harkened to by the unnamed teacher of Ecclesiastes.

> Have you not known? Have you not heard? The LORD is the everlasting God, the Creator of the ends of the earth.

He does not faint or grow weary; his understanding is unsearchable. He gives power to the faint, and to him who has no might he increases strength. Even youths shall faint and be weary, and young men shall fall exhausted; but they who wait for the LORD shall renew their strength; they shall mount up with wings like eagles; they shall run and not be weary; they shall walk and not faint

(Isaiah 40:28-31).

Not by might nor by power but by God's Spirit. The best that youth can offer will not suffice. The strength of youth may be able to hold the branch to keep himself from falling to his death in the valley below a bit longer than the aged can, but it's just a matter of time before that grip will weaken and fail. The mouth of the grave gapes open below all who breathe and we cannot escape its jaws. God offers hope as he directs us away from self-effort to him who is mighty in power and mighty to save.

True and enduring physical fitness are found not in a personal trainer but in the personal Saviour, in whom the reality of the vanity observed by the Preacher is swallowed up in victory. Hear the declaration of victory posted by the apostle as he describes the ultimate makeover.

I tell you this, brothers: flesh and blood cannot inherit the kingdom of God, nor does the perishable inherit the imperishable. Behold! I tell you a mystery. We shall not all sleep, but we shall all be changed, in a moment, in the twinkling of an eye, at the last trumpet. For the trumpet will sound, and the dead will be raised imperishable, and we shall be changed. For this perishable body must put on the imperishable, and this mortal body must put on immortality. When the perishable puts on the imperishable, and the mortal puts on immortality, then shall come to pass the saying that is written: 'Death is swallowed up in victory.' 'O death, where is your victory? O death, where is your sting?' The sting of death is sin, and the power of sin is the law. But thanks be to God, who gives us the victory through our Lord Jesus Christ

(1 Corinthians 15:50-57).

That's why Paul can say:

For I consider that the sufferings of this present time are not worth comparing with the glory that is to be revealed to us … For we know that the whole creation has been groaning together in the pains of childbirth until now. And not only the creation, but we ourselves, who have the firstfruits of the Spirit, groan inwardly as we wait eagerly for adoption as sons, the redemption of our bodies

(Romans 8:18-23).

Fallen reality of life under the sun becomes transformed, infused with life, hope and meaning.

So we do not lose heart. Though our outer nature is wasting away, our inner nature is being renewed day by day. For this slight momentary affliction is preparing for us an eternal weight of glory beyond all comparison, as we look not to the things that are seen but to the things that are unseen. For the things that are seen are transient, but the things that are unseen are eternal

(2 Corinthians 4:16-18).

That's 'above the sun' talk. That's talk full of life and hope because it trusts in Christ and believes the one who sent him. That's the perspective of redemptive realism.

Vanity of strength and beauty

In Christ all things are made new. While physical beauty and care of one's health are good, genuine strength and real beauty are not found in outward appearance but in Christ and the working of his Spirit in our inner being. Peter directs our attention to the concern of a redemptive makeover as we grow in grace, experiencing the sanctifying scalpel of the Holy Spirit as ones no longer dead in sin but alive in Christ.

> Do not let your adorning be external — the braiding of hair, the wearing of gold, or the putting on of clothing — but let your adorning be the hidden person of the heart with the imperishable beauty of a gentle and quiet spirit, which in God's sight is very precious
>
> (1 Peter 3:3-4).

Old Testament saints, such as Sarah, Ruth or Hannah, may not adorn the cover of *Cosmopolitan*, but they would grace the portrait gallery of God's favour.

As I mentioned, I belong to the YMCA. I admit that one reason I joined was to do battle with the effects of time and the forces of gravity. I wanted to keep my stomach a six-pack rather than allowing it to become a keg. I wanted to remind my testosterone-deprived muscles that I knew they were there, rather than allowing them to drift into the obscurity of flaccidity. There's nothing wrong with that, as long as misplaced hope or misdirected notions do not drive the endeavour. Paul admits as much, but he also leads us to a gym arrived at by fearing God and keeping his commandments.

> ...train yourself for godliness; for while bodily training is of some value, godliness is of value in every way, as it holds promise for the present life and also for the life to come
>
> (1 Timothy 4:7-8).

'Train' translates the Greek word from which we derive the term 'gymnasium'. It gives new meaning to the call of Philippians 2:12-13 to 'work out your own salvation with fear and trembling, for it is God who works in you...' The workout of God's gym is the regimen of godliness sculpted to the image of Christ, strong in the strength of Christ, adorned with the beauty of Christ.

Jim, the guy with the protruding intestines, refused to stop working out, torn abs and all. But it was more than his muscles being defined. Rather, he allowed himself to be defined by his muscles. Muscle mass was his identity. It was his life.

The life of a young woman with perhaps the same penchant as Jim took quite a different course as God led her from futility to fear of him. Joni Eareckson was born in Baltimore, Maryland, in 1950. She was the youngest of four sisters. Joni had it all — a loving family, athleticism, beauty, popularity. But the July after she graduated from high school something happened that changed her life.

She was to meet her sister Kathy and some friends on the shore of the Chesapeake Bay to swim. When she arrived, she jumped right in. Joni now tells the story.

One hot July afternoon in 1967, I dove into a shallow lake and my life changed for ever. I suffered a spinal cord fracture that left me paralyzed from the neck down, without use of my hands and legs. Lying in my hospital bed, I tried desperately to make sense of the horrible turn of events. I begged friends to assist me in suicide. Slit my wrists, dump pills down my throat, anything to end my misery!

I had so many questions. I believed in God, but I was angry with Him. How could my circumstance be a demonstration of His love and power? Surely He could have stopped it from happening. How can permanent, lifelong paralysis be a part of His loving plan for me? Unless I found answers, I didn't see how this God could be worthy of my trust.

Steve, a friend of mine, took on my questions. He pointed me to Christ.

Now I believe that God's purpose in my accident was to turn a stubborn kid into a woman who would reflect patience, endurance and a lively, optimistic hope of the heavenly glories above

(from Joni's web site).

Paradoxically, that event in 1967 saved Joni's life. It brought her to Jesus Christ for salvation and gave her a life in knowing and serving him. Joni Eareckson (now Tada), a quadriplegic confined to a wheelchair, today is an internationally known artist who paints with the brush in her mouth, a talented vocalist, a radio host, an author of seventeen books and an advocate for disabled persons worldwide. Her physical state serves as a parable of one losing her life that she might gain it.

Under the sun Joni had lost it all by our culture's standards. It was when God lifted her eyes above the sun to see him, and by his grace led her to gain Christ that she found beauty that will not fade with age and she can look forward to a resurrected body free from the ravages of life under the sun.

The Bible says our bodies are temples. We go along with that, but do we believe they are temples *of the Holy Spirit* — vessels holding the treasure of the gospel of Christ, jars of clay where God lives by his Spirit? Or do we believe that our bodies are just temples — like those empty, hulking church buildings dotting the European landscape in need of maintenance, hawking souvenirs, temples occupied by no god but self? May God grant us a firm grip on redemptive reality that honours and serves him in our mortal bodies, where we as the Bride of Christ, live out the words: 'Charm is deceitful, and beauty is vain, but a woman who fears the LORD is to be praised' (Prov. 31:30).

Questions from Qoheleth

1. What observations does the Preacher make about youth in Ecclesiastes 11:9-10? Why would he draw the conclusions he does?
2. What does the image of youth convey? How does that image epitomize the illusion and hopelessness of life that saturates the Preacher's journal?
3. How can we go overboard when it comes to the pursuit of youth? What balance is called for? What weighs each side of the scale to achieve this balance? How does Proverbs 20:29 refer to this balance?
4. What blessing of aging does the Bible give for the individual and the community (e.g., Prov. 16:31; 1 Peter 5:1-5)? According to Psalm 77, what thread spans the continuum of aging?
5. Unpack the vivid portrayal of aging in Ecclesiastes 12:1-7, describing the observations and images, and summarizing the conclusions of the Preacher. What is your attitude toward the elderly? How does that attitude line up with God's view of the aged?
6. What are some of the popular views about death? In this world under the sun, what place does death have (cf. Gen. 2:17)? In what way does death validate the Preacher's view of vanity?
7. What redemptive reality related to death is ours in Christ (cf. 1 Cor. 15:50-57)? How does that escape from the bond of death become ours (John 5:25; Rom. 6:23)? What does a life derailed from the terminus of the grave look like (cf. Rom. 8:18-23; 2 Cor. 4:16-18)?
8. How does Paul explain in 1 Thessalonians 4:13 - 5:11 that the Christian's hope is not a chasing after wind? Where does he show this hope under the sun, yet beyond the sun? How does the resurrection life of Christ in which we participate by grace lay siege to all the vanities of life, infusing them with enduring value?

But whatever gain I had, I counted as loss for the sake of Christ. Indeed, I count everything as loss because of the surpassing worth of knowing Christ Jesus my Lord. For his sake I have suffered the loss of all things and count them as rubbish, in order that I may gain Christ and be found in him, not having a righteousness of my own that comes from the law, but that which comes through faith in Christ, the righteousness from God that depends on faith — that I may know him and the power of his resurrection, and may share his sufferings, becoming like him in his death, that by any means possible I may attain the resurrection from the dead

(Philippians 3:7-11).

10.
Bonfire of the vanities

Bonfire of the Vanities was a highly acclaimed 1987 novel by Tom Wolfe made into a lowly acclaimed 1990 movie. 'Bonfire of the Vanities' actually refers to a historical event that took place on 7 February 1497 in Florence, Italy, when thousands of objects and books considered vulgar were collected and publicly burned. The expression 'bonfire of the vanities' refers to the burning of objects that are deemed occasions for sin.

That's pretty much what God's purpose is for us in the book of Ecclesiastes. There are those things and activities in our lives — family, friends, relationships, money, possessions, alcohol, sex, TV, internet, intelligence, academic degrees, religious activity, social causes, physical appearance and all kinds of other things and activities in this fallen world under the sun — that can become objects of desire and occasions for sin. Not that these things are necessarily bad in themselves, but they become bad when they are misused or take the place of God — either as objects of our devotion or sources for what only God can give.

Every one of us wrestles with this misalignment of foolishness to one degree or another, where we either attempt to be as God, trying to gain control or deciding for ourselves what is good or evil. We can also make something to be God, looking to it for what only God can give and giving our affections to it, where it becomes a seductress for us, enticing us to ruin. Either way, the challenge God lays before us has to do with idolatry, those things in our lives where we try to find salvation, significance, security, solace and ultimate satisfaction in created things rather than the Creator who is to ever be praised.

We've seen that the bulk of Ecclesiastes contains the ponderings of a religious observer to life, someone named 'the Preacher'. He is called the 'Preacher' but not in the sense of one expositing the Word of God, but more as a collector of thoughts on life, expounding on the mettle and merit of candidates for meaning, purpose and value in the world's marketplace. The perspective from which he makes his observations is 'under the sun' and what he sees is not very encouraging. The race is not to the swift. The good die young. The young will die.

The ponderings of the Preacher are framed by another teacher, one not named. He speaks about what the Preacher has said. Only his perspective looks beyond the sun to the God who is and who reigns and who has spoken. He affirms the Preacher's observations, but he says that there's more to it than meets the eye. His counsel to fear God and follow his commandments touches on and transforms every aspect of life.

As we bring our survey of Ecclesiastes to a close, trying to make sanity out of an often contradictory, confusing and empty existence, we want to make sure we take with us the life-directing, life-changing message God has for us as we live with and for him in this world under the sun, looking for the world to come. We can summarize the contrast of the book under two headings: life under the sun, and life under the Son.

Life under the sun

We've seen in our study of Ecclesiastes certain phrases that capture the futility of life in a fallen world: 'under the sun', 'striving after the wind'. But none captures the tone better than the opening words of the Preacher: 'Vanity of vanities, says the Preacher, vanity of vanities! All is vanity' (Eccles. 1:2).

'Vanity' does not indicate conceit, although we've seen the gravitational pull of self-glory, self-service and self-reliance under the sun. Rather, the Preacher's 'vanity' points to meaningless, empty, pointless, fruitless. Everything, he says, is vanity. He can find nothing of redeeming value. And then he goes on in his chronicle of observations to comment on just about everything life has to offer.

What is the Preacher saying — that nothing in this fallen world under the sun is worthwhile, that nothing has value or merit? He sends a mixed message. At one point he says righteousness is a good thing. Later he says not to be overly righteous. At one point he says money offers no real security. Later he says, 'Money answers everything.' He seems conflicted. On the one hand he says sex, possessions, youth, government and religion are all gifts or provisions of God for our good and enjoyment. On the other hand, he says they are all dead ends and sources of inevitable disappointment. Then, with a shrug of the shoulders, he says, 'You might as well enjoy these things while you can. At least they'll take the edge off your miserable life.'

If we read these things looking for inspiration, we're in big trouble. But if we read them for honest assessment of life, we recognize the truth in his observations. Life doesn't work like it should. We have trouble reconciling suffering and injustice with a God who's supposed to be all good, all wise and all powerful. Things appear to be no different for Christians who are supposed to be loved by God than they are for non-Christians who couldn't care less about God and oppose him to his face. You can hear how jaded, sceptical, cynical and fatalistic the Preacher is in his observations:

> There is an evil that I have seen under the sun, and it lies heavy on mankind: a man to whom God gives wealth, possessions, and honour, so that he lacks nothing of all that he desires, yet God does not give him power to enjoy them, but a stranger enjoys them. This is vanity; it is a grievous evil. If a man fathers a hundred children and lives many years, so that the days of his years are many, but his soul is not satisfied with life's good things, and he also has no burial, I say that a stillborn child is better off than he. For it comes in vanity and goes in darkness, and in darkness its name is covered. Moreover, it has not seen the sun or known anything, yet it finds rest rather than he. Even though he should live a thousand years twice over, yet enjoy no good — do not all go to the one place?
>
> All the toil of man is for his mouth, yet his appetite is not satisfied. For what advantage has the wise man over the fool? And what does the poor man have who knows how to conduct himself before the living? Better is the sight of the eyes than the wandering of the appetite: this also is vanity and a striving after wind.
>
> Whatever has come to be has already been named, and it is known what man is, and that he is not able to dispute with one stronger than he. The more words, the more vanity, and what is the advantage to man?
>
> (Eccles. 6:1-11).

The conflicting message observed by the Preacher hits home — sometimes pretty hard. If we are honest with ourselves in the reality we observe, we'll agree with the Preacher's assessment — vanity of vanities.

Jerram Barrs, a former student of Francis Schaeffer, describes the impact of the book of Ecclesiastes on him as a non-Christian, and in so doing, captures for us the impact of the book's dynamic realized through the interaction of the two takes on life afforded by the Preacher and redemptively recast by the unnamed teacher.

> Within a few days of meeting Mike, he invited me to a Bible study in his apartment. I don't think he knew at the time just how appropriate his text was for me, but God led him to give a study on the first two chapters of the book of Ecclesiastes. He began by reading the following passage: 'Vanity of vanities, says the Preacher, vanity of vanities! All is vanity.' He carried on and read those first two chapters in their entirety. I was amazed. Until that moment it had never occurred to me that the Bible is a book about life, that it addresses the deep questions of the human dilemma. Just like most non-Christians in the modern western world, I had always thought of the Bible as a 'religious book'. But I had never thought of it as a book that speaks to the questions all have about our existence, our needs, our problems, a book that answers these questions. It was as if Ecclesiastes was written for me and was speaking directly to me.

As he touches on the urgent need for us to be addressed by Ecclesiastes, Barrs then brings home to us the need for truth to allow us to make sanity out of vanity, a truth that does not necessarily answer all our questions or resolve our confusion, but a truth bound up in the God who is and who has spoken — and a faith that embraces it.

I have since found that it is a book that speaks to many modern and particularly to postmodern people simply because it is so direct about the futility wrapped up in the human condition. It pulls no punches but rather acknowledges the sense of emptiness that pervades so much of life in a fallen world. It offers partial healing for the wounds we feel, but this healing is not given easily or lightly, nor as if the medicine applied to us will wipe away all our tears in the present time. This sober realism in Ecclesiastes was God's means of convincing me to take his Word seriously and to begin to consider his Word as words of truth, truth that makes sense of the world in which we live, truth that fits like a glove on the hand of reality

(Barrs, *The Heart of Evangelism*, p. 121f.).

Ecclesiastes is not intended to make us pessimists, although it contains the warning of bondage to pessimism for those constrained by a perspective that reaches no higher than the fallen created order under the sun. As Barrs observes, God gives us the book because he wants to make us realists, seeing a world that is a mess and seeing people failing to find some sense of hope and life and meaning in that mess. But the message is that there's more, and that more comes to us by lifting our eyes beyond the pale of this world to the God who reigns on high and who has entered our world under the sun to bring hope, a God who makes sanity out of vanity.

Life under the Son

For I consider that the sufferings of this present time are not worth comparing with the glory that is to be revealed to us. For the creation waits with eager longing

for the revealing of the sons of God. For the creation
was subjected to futility, not willingly, but because of
him who subjected it, in hope that the creation itself
will be set free from its bondage to decay and obtain
the freedom of the glory of the children of God. For
we know that the whole creation has been groaning
together in the pains of childbirth until now. And not
only the creation, but we ourselves, who have the
firstfruits of the Spirit, groan inwardly as we wait eagerly
for adoption as sons, the redemption of our bodies. For
in this hope we were saved. Now hope that is seen is not
hope. For who hopes for what he sees? But if we hope
for what we do not see, we wait for it with patience
(Romans 8:18-25).

Into this world under the sun subjected to futility, God sent
his Son to redeem not only a people for his own possession
but to redeem a fallen created order. One day, the Son will
come again, upon which time all things will be made new. The
old order of things will pass away; the new will be ushered
in. It is in this new redemptive order of Christ's achievement
that hope is found and that the vain things of this world are
renewed in Christ.

Amidst the confusion that besets us in this dysfunctional
life, we rest in God for our hope and cry out to him in our
need. The apostle Paul who declares the redemption of the
created order above goes on to equip us for prayer in our
sojourning (Rom. 8:26-27), encouraging us to press on in the
knowledge of God's redemptive hand.

And we know that for those who love God all things
work together for good, for those who are called
according to his purpose. For those whom he foreknew
he also predestined to be conformed to the image of

his Son, in order that he might be the firstborn among
many brothers

(Rom. 8:28-29).

In other words, we might not be able to make head nor tail of
all that happens in this world, but we entrust ourselves to our
faithful Creator, confident in his purpose, content in his arms.
By fearing God and hearing and applying his Word, we find
our footing amidst the sinking sands of finding life and hope
in the wares of Vanity Fair. Even our prayer itself becomes
invigorated by confidence in God rather than the futility
engendered by the vanity of prayer that does not fear him but
seeks to manipulate God or operate without him.

Paul finishes his thought in Romans 8 by driving home
the ground of the firm foundation of the Christian's hope
residing in the election of God and the resurrection victory
of the crucified Christ and work of the Spirit who secures us
to Christ. He points us to the redemptive truth that belies the
instability and insanity the Preacher of Ecclesiastes observes
under the sun, the knowledge of which gives us bearings,
mitigates the frustration and compels our journey under the
withering heat of sun of a fallen world.

No, in all these things we are more than conquerors
through him who loved us. For I am sure that neither
death nor life, nor angels nor rulers, nor things present
nor things to come, nor powers, nor height nor depth,
nor anything else in all creation, will be able to separate
us from the love of God in Christ Jesus our Lord

(Rom. 8:37-39).

Paul is saying that nothing in the created order, fallen as it is,
can separate us from the Creator in his redemptive love for us

realized in Jesus Christ. Right in the thick of Paul's discourse, we hear pessimistic echoes of the Preacher.

> Who shall separate us from the love of Christ? Shall tribulation, or distress, or persecution, or famine, or nakedness, or danger, or sword? As it is written, 'For your sake we are being killed all the day long; we are regarded as sheep to be slaughtered'
>
> (Rom. 8:35-36).

In this world we will have trouble, our Lord Jesus guaranteed us. But take heart, he has overcome the world. The Preacher's observations are right. The world is a hard place — inhospitable, unpredictable, devoid of hope. He makes realists of us. The unnamed teacher, however, directs us to a right view of God and directs us to listen to him. As we incline our ear, he tells us the story of Jesus and invites us to come to him that we might have life and have it abundantly.

Our enemy the devil, the proprietor of this fallen age, takes us through the mall of Vanity Fair (open year round with the world's empty offerings) and displays the wares of the world. He presses the question, 'Which one suits your desire?' Our question needs to be, 'Isn't there another?' So we turn to the voice of the living and true God and he points us to Jesus. 'This is my beloved Son, with whom I am well pleased. Listen to him.' And as we give ear to this Son of God's love, he tells us the world makes great boasts and offers great promises, but in his beloved Son is life: abundant, full and free. Jesus prays for our protection and guidance in our sojourning under the sun.

> I have given them your word, and the world has hated them because they are not of the world, just as I am not

of the world. I do not ask that you take them out of the world, but that you keep them from the evil one. They are not of the world, just as I am not of the world. Sanctify them in the truth; your word is truth. As you sent me into the world, so I have sent them into the world. And for their sake I consecrate myself, that they also may be sanctified in truth

(John 17:14-19).

Coming to Jesus belongs not just to the outset of the Christian life, but to daily confrontations with the suffering, injustices, darkness, despair, disappointment, deprivation, death and all those other hallmarks of the fallen world in which we live that we encounter day in and day out. The vanities for the bonfire include not only those things we trust for life but those things we might substitute for the God we are to glorify and enjoy, which allows us to sanctify all those things.

Basically, the book of Ecclesiastes vies for our hearts as it takes into account each offering of life. The message is not just to unbelievers to listen to God and come to Christ, but to us as believers who are prone to wander, prone to leave the God we love by operating according to the ways and means of this fallen world, walking by sight rather than by faith. That's why the epistles are filled with admonitions to live by faith, operating in the perspective and power of new life in Christ. Those admonitions address us as Christians to live as redemptive realists. God speaks to protect us from the futility of finding our ultimate delight in created things and to beckon us to himself.

Were you surprised in our survey of the book how virtually every area of life was addressed — family, friends, relationships, money, possessions, alcohol, sex, entertainment, intelligence, academic degrees, religious activity, social causes, physical appearance? Every one of these things can become for us an idol and be stationed in the battleground of our hearts. God places a warning label on each one of them, alerting us to danger. He wants to protect us from lies and disappointments and false hopes. Also on that label is found the inscription 'made by God' for enjoyment and provision in our journey under the sun. Under that inscription are instructions for proper use to which the unnamed teacher calls our attention — 'Fear God and keep his commandments.'

Family, money, sex, social causes — all these things are sanctified as we receive them with thanksgiving from the hand of God and honour him in them all — how our family relationships reflect his love and design, how we use our goods knowing they are really his, that safe sex is sex within the boundaries of his commands. The breadth of subject matter in the book of Ecclesiastes impresses this upon us — that there is nowhere and no thing in which we are not to fear God and keep his commands.

Our God wants our whole hearts, our full allegiance, our undiluted devotion, our rapt attention, our unwavering trust. Of those things that compete for our hearts that we place before our eyes, Jesus asks, 'Do you love me more than these?' He bids us to gather up the idols he has unearthed and the good things we have defiled by sin that he has pointed out through the inventory of our lives taken in the study of Ecclesiastes, take them to the bonfire set by the Spirit of truth and throw them on its pyre to destroy or to refine, with this goal — that Jesus Christ might be our life, our love, our Lord.

> Forbid it, Lord, that I should boast,
> Save in the death of Christ my God:
> All the vain things that charm me most,
> I sacrifice them to his blood.
> ('When I Survey the Wondrous Cross', Isaac Watts)

Questions from Qoheleth

1. How would you summarize God's pastoral purpose in the book of Ecclesiastes? How does that message speak to unbelievers under the sun? How does that message speak to believers under the sun?

2. In what way does Ecclesiastes make us realists? Redemptive realists? How does redemptive realism enable us to press on with joy and expectation in the hardships and confusion and religious contradiction we experience in life, not merely to cope but with hope?

3. Give concrete examples for how we might try to find salvation, significance, security, solace or ultimate satisfaction in created things rather than the Creator. Why are these efforts futile?

4. Are we to heap all the Preacher surveys on the bonfire as the vanities he sees them to be? If not, what about the offerings of life to be purged by fire that they might find proper place and use in our lives?

5. How does Paul answer the Preacher in Romans 8:1-39? Where do you see echoes of the expressions used by the Preacher to characterize life in a fallen world?

6. How do fearing God and keeping his commandments come into play in the dynamics of Romans 8? How is this reflected in Jesus' high priestly prayer in John 17:1-26?

7. In what way does God vie for our hearts through the message of Ecclesiastes? How is this expressed in passages like Deuteronomy 5:28 - 6:16; Ezekiel 14:1-5; and Matthew 22:34-40?

Then I saw a new heaven and a new earth, for the first heaven and the first earth had passed away, and the sea was no more. And I saw the holy city, new Jerusalem, coming down out of heaven from God, prepared as a bride adorned for her husband. And I heard a loud voice from the throne saying, 'Behold, the dwelling place of God is with man. He will dwell with them, and they will be his people, and God himself will be with them as their God. He will wipe away every tear from their eyes, and death shall be no more, neither shall there be mourning nor crying nor pain any more, for the former things have passed away.'

And he who was seated on the throne said, 'Behold, I am making all things new.' Also he said, 'Write this down, for these words are trustworthy and true'

(Revelation 21:1-5).

Conclusion
— Verity of verities

What is the opposite of vanity? If we take the common definition of the word, the one that first occurs to us, we might think humility is vanity's antonym. Certainly, humility is consistent with the lesson plan of Ecclesiastes as we are brought to the fear of God, regarding him in his greatness and ourselves in the limitations of our createdness, particularly with our skewed perspective and arrogant heart. In humility we set aside our pretensions, even our aspirations and lay our all at the feet of our God, saying, 'Not to us, not to us, O Lord, but to you be the glory.' 'Not my will but your will be done.' Humility looks in the mirror and sees the image-bearer of God that reflects his glory and ownership and acts accordingly.

But the second definition of vanity, the one employed in the book of Ecclesiastes, has more to do with emptiness, futility and meaninglessness. It has a ring of ineffectiveness, with an echo of senselessness. When my children were young another family and mine went on a hike around a large bay. Hiking with small children is never easy but this one ended up in a category of its own. I later called it 'hell hike'. It all started out rather innocuously. Before long, however, things went downhill; and by that I mean uphill. To make a long trek short, we came to a cliff, staring up with great misgiving at its steep incline. Weak and weary at this point, we had to get up that cliff guiding a group of little children. The other husband and I laboured with great exertion at the climb and trepidation at the danger below. Here's the reason I relate this story. The face of the cliff in front of me was dotted with clumps of grass and small branches, inviting me like gripping stones on a climbing wall to take hold and make progress. However, whenever I would take hold of one it would promptly pull loose. Like clouds without water, they were a vain offering, holding out promise and hope but thoroughly ineffective for anything but peril. Those branches that were firmly rooted I discovered were filled with thorns and defied helpfulness. We did survive 'hell hike', but no thanks to those empty offerings.

Ecclesiastes makes it clear to us that what we need are not vanities, with their empty promises and dead ends, which often cause pain and sorrow. What we need are verities, truths, something we can count on to find help for today and hope for tomorrow.

'Vanity' means empty, meaningless. 'Verity' means truth and substance. Vanity is a chasing after wind. Verity is arriving at what can be trusted. And that's exactly what God wants us to see through the interaction of the two figures of Ecclesiastes. There is a place where verity can be found, but like searching for water in a lush garden rather than an arid desert, we need to know where to look. The world has offerings of hope and meaning and identity and salvation, but God makes it clear that our hope is not found under the sun in anything the world has to offer. Our hope is found in God and the hope God provides is found in Jesus Christ.

Life under the sun can be onerous, the sun beating down upon us, draining us of strength, mirages of meaning goading us on, only to disappoint when we arrive at their empty promise. However, the redemptive lesson plan always teaches us of sure and certain provision of God in Christ.

170

- Salvation is not in good works that would put God in my debt, but in Christ where God has provided a righteousness that is by grace alone through faith alone in Christ alone. The justice the Preacher seeks is realized in the cross. The righteousness the Preacher values is provided in the Christ.
- Significance is not in academics or in any other mantle we might don at our society's behest, but in Christ. We can find no greater accolade than that we are a child of God, our standing based on the credentials of Christ. The name the Preacher sought to preserve through accomplishments and monuments is given us inviolably through being united to Jesus Christ.
- Security is not in a bank account, but in Christ. In him are found the immeasurable riches of God's grace, riches not subject to the whims of the stock market. Our inheritance in Christ is held for us without depletion and, in God's electing hand, we are held for it. The protection of money touted by the Preacher will fail, but provision of our God for this life and that to come will not and cannot.
- Solace is not in a bottle that drowns our sorrows, but in Christ. In Christ, we can face the trouble, trials and travails of life under the sun. In him we enjoy a peace that surpasses understanding, a peace the world does not know and has no right to, a peace we hold out as ambassadors of Christ. The ways advocated by the Preacher to numb the harshness and to mask the insanity of life under the sun are redemptively extended to us in Christ, who will not break a bruised reed nor snuff out a smouldering wick.
- Ultimate satisfaction is not found in temporary pleasures, but in knowing and loving Christ, and doing what he commands. Christ is our delight. Christ is our boast. Christ is our peace. When Jesus says he came to bring life and that abundantly, he resolves the angst felt by the Preacher and is the goal of the counsel of the unnamed teacher in fearing God and hearing and heeding his voice.

All these verities we can count on, because Jesus is *the* Verity — the way, the truth, the life.

To be bound up in Christ is to live in redemptive reality, to live in and live out a Christo-centric life. Copernicus posited a helio-centric solar system, where the earth revolves around the sun rather than the converse. By its place in a Book that records a redemptive history and speaks of Christ in all its parts, Ecclesiastes puts forth a Christo-centric existence where our lives revolve around the Son, receiving warmth and light and cheer and stability in him.

A Son-centred existence redeems life under the sun, removing the wares of Vanity Fair from improper use and restoring them to their place, using them as God intended, for his glory, received with gratitude from his hand, regulated by his commandments.

Living as redemptive realists means:

- expecting the world not to make sense because of the ravages of the Fall and our limited and skewed perspectives as fallen people;
- living by faith in a God who rules and reigns and works out his perfect purposes in all that comes to pass, a God whom we fashion not according to the conclusions we might draw from our forensic observations under the sun but whom we understand according to his self-revelation given us in his Word;
- looking to a day when all things will be made new where the creation subjected to futility will pass away, knowing that God's plan is not just for a redeemed people but for a redeemed cosmos;
- redeeming the time, living out the redemptive admonition communicated by Paul for those in the world but not of it: 'Look carefully then how you walk, not as unwise but as wise, making the best use of the time, because the days are

evil. Therefore do not be foolish, but understand what the will of the Lord is' (Ephesians 5:15-17);

- walking according to Christ rather than to the way that seems right in our own eyes, according to the hollow and deceptive philosophy of this age, according to the traditions of men and the base principles of this world, concerned not with pragmatics but with the love of obedience;
- admitting the pain and senselessness of the life but resting in God's salve and solution in Christ, trusting that in the mind of God resides the answer and rationale to give sanity to what seems to us a confusing life;
- pressing on to work and serve knowing that our labour in the Lord is not in vain, despite appearances of futility to the contrary.

The book of Ecclesiastes doesn't answer all our questions. In fact, it makes a point of raising questions we cannot answer, highlighting our limitations and inadequacies, displaying life's frustrations and inconsistencies. Ecclesiastes exposes us as created beings as it sets us up for a radical reorientation to life. It brings us to an end of ourselves that we might learn to fear God and keep his commandments, to trust and obey, come what may. It shows us ways we oppose God, substitute for God, run and hide from God. Like a child finds refuge and peace in the presence of its father, so Ecclesiastes takes our hand and enfolds it in the hand of our heavenly Father as we negotiate the busy highways of life, not understanding a whole lot, but glorifying and enjoying him who does.

Norwegian artist Edvard Munch (1863-1944) vividly captures the angst of life. His most famous work, *The Scream*, depicts a freeze frame of life that assaults the viewer with uncontrolled volatility. The long, multi-directional, wavy lines convey a world in disorder, disarray and turmoil. The red hues of the sky speak not to the beauty of the setting sun, but to the panic induced by a tumultuous world that tyrannizes us. The haunting figure to which the eye is drawn can do nothing but cover his ears and scream. But the scream is silent. Is there anyone to hear? Is there anyone to help?

The figure in *The Scream* is simply responding to what he sees. And what he sees is life assaulting him. He cannot control things. They are more than he can manage. He cannot make sense of things.

I can think of no better representation of the Old Testament book of Ecclesiastes than Munch's *The Scream*. When we look at life 'under the sun', the refrain of the book, we are driven to conclude that all is but a vapour. 'Vanity of vanities! All is vanity.' Empty, pointless, meaningless, fleeting, oppressive, unfair, insane. As much as we try to dig ourselves out of a hole, the walls collapse and we are left to dig and dig still more. Along with Munch's open-mouthed, ear-covered, isolated, haunting figure, we can look at life that is hostile, oppressive and relentless, and the only voice we can muster is a scream (adapted from *The Prayer of Jehoshaphat*, p. 83f.).

This is where the Preacher would leave us. The unnamed teacher, however, affirms the Preacher's observation and agrees with his conclusions, but only if the fallen world is the final answer. But it's not. God is; and he has intervened in his love and mercy and grace. He sent his beloved Son under the sun to redeem those under the sun that all who trust in him should not perish but have everlasting life, a life that colours and sustains us each and every day as we sojourn under the sun.

The operating system urged upon us by our God to make us redemptive realists is summed up by the apostle Paul and with it we close.

Oh, the depth of the riches and wisdom and knowledge of God! How unsearchable are his judgements and how inscrutable his ways! 'For who has known the mind of the Lord, or who has been his counsellor?' 'Or who has given a gift to him that he might be repaid?' For from him and through him and to him are all things. To him be glory for ever. Amen

(Romans 11:33-36).

Amen and amen.

Questions from Qoheleth

1. How does 'hell hike' illustrate the Preacher's quest and observations? What parallels have you found in your life's journey to this point?
2. In a redemptive framework, what is the difference between a vanity and a verity? In this sense what would be a vanity of vanities? A verity of verities? What is the origin of vanities? Of verities? How do these origins relate to the message of the unnamed teacher as he addresses the observations of the Preacher?
3. In contrast to the vain offerings of the world, what verities are found in Jesus Christ in respect to the following:
    a. Salvation (John 14:6)
    b. Significance (1 John 3:1-3)
    c. Security (John 10:27-30)
    d. Solace (John 14:27)
    e. Ultimate satisfaction (John 6:35)
4. Paul distinguishes between vanity and verity, rock and sinking sand, in 1 Corinthians 15. What is the subject of this chapter and how does it provide a ground for faith? What are the various aspects Paul addresses in respect to vanity (see 1 Cor. 15:2, 10, 14, 58)? How does this encourage you in your Christian faith, hope and love as you live under the sun?
5. Explain what it means to live as a redemptive realist. How does this redemptive realism work itself out in a confusing situation in your life? How does this affect your life's ambitions?

6. Ecclesiastes doesn't answer all our questions or relieve all our angst but it does give us the framework in which to handle these things. What is that framework? How is this framework represented in passages like Romans 11:33-36? From what perplexity does this doxology in Romans flow that reflects the Preacher's vantage point?

7. In what way does Munch's *The Scream* capture the Preacher's observations under the sun? What would you add to that painting to introduce the redemptive perspective brought by the unnamed teacher?

8. What happens to the world under the sun in Revelation 21:1-8 and 22:1-6? What message of hope does Revelation extend that the unnamed teacher extends in Ecclesiastes?